the
vietnamese
collection

hamlyn

AUTHOR'S ACKNOWLEDGEMENTS

Love and thanks to David Brown, Gabrielle Mander and my family. Many thanks too to Andy Davey and Clare Newson of Mosaics Restaurant in Yoxford, Suffolk, for their enthusiastic help and for allowing me the use of their kitchen.

First published in 2000 by Hamlyn a division of Octopus Publishing Group Ltd, 2–4 Heron Quays, London E14 4JP

This paperback edition first published 2002

Copyright © 2000, 2002 Octopus Publishing Group Ltd.

Distributed in the United States and Canada by
Sterling Publishing Co., Inc.
387 Park Avenue South, New York, NY 10016-8810

British Library Cataloguing-in-Publication Data
A catalogue record for this book is available from the British Library

ISBN 0 600 60593 0

Printed in China

Notes:
Both metric and imperial measures have been given in all recipes. Use one set of measurements only and not a mixture of both.

Standard level spoon measurements are used in all recipes:
1 tablespoon = one 15 ml spoon
1 teaspoon = one 5 ml spoon

Eggs should be large unless otherwise stated.

Milk should be full fat unless otherwise stated.

Pepper should be freshly ground black unless otherwise stated.

Fresh herbs should be used unless otherwise stated. If unavailable, use dried herbs as an alternative but halve the given quantities.

Fresh chillies should be used unless otherwise stated.

Nuts and nut derivatives. This book includes dishes made with nuts and nut derivatives. It is advisable for customers with known allergic reactions to nuts and nut derivatives and those who may be potentially vulnerable to these allergies, such as pregnant and nursing mothers, invalids, the elderly, babies and children, to avoid dishes made with nuts and nut oils. It is also prudent to check the labels of pre-prepared ingredients for the possible inclusion of nut derivatives.

Ovens should be preheated to the specified temperature – if using a fan assisted oven, follow the manufacturer's instructions for adjusting the time and temperature.

Jackum Brown

photography by Ian Wallace

contents

introduction

Vietnam is a long, narrow country squeezed between Laos and Cambodia to the west, the South China Sea to the east and south, and dominated by the enormous bulk of China to the north. Vietnam has been heavily influenced by China over the course of the centuries, but in its food, as well as all the other aspects of its life, it has made its own traditions and created a distinctive cuisine in its own right.

The country divides geographically into three parts: the fertile Red River delta in the north, surrounded by wild hills and mountains on three sides; the central and southern highlands; and in the south, the watery landscape of the Mekong delta, perfect for rice growing. Not surprisingly, north and south Vietnamese people differ from one another. Not only because of historical, political and geographical reasons, but also culturally. This difference is reflected in the cuisines, although rice is the staple food throughout Vietnam, and rice noodles are also extremely popular.

Hanoi in the north, Hué in the centre and Ho Chi Minh (formerly Saigon) in the south, all have their speciality cuisines, but Ho Chi Minh is thought to be the food capital of the country. Monosodium glutamate (MSG) is widely used, particularly in the north, although some restaurants in tourist centres are beginning to realize that many foreigners prefer not to eat it, and advertise accordingly.

Stir-fried food originated in China, and, of all the countries in South-east Asia, only Vietnam uses chopsticks to eat with. The food in the north is the most similar to Chinese food, and the least varied. Central Vietnamese food tends to be hotter, using more chilli and less black pepper for heat. There is still plenty of game available in the highlands – wild boar, pheasants and so on – which appears on the table whenever possible. Southern cuisine tends to be the most varied, with both Indian and French influences at work. The French introduced asparagus and strawberries; the Indians curry spices and potatoes.

The Vietnamese wrap up much of their food in fresh salad leaves, with fresh herbs tucked inside as well. This is a perfect example of the individuality of their cuisine, as it is thought to be a custom of the original inhabitants of the area, that is, before the Chinese began their 1,000 years of direct rule, which ended in AD 938.

The food in Vietnam is not, generally speaking, very chilli-hot. It is quite subtle in its use of herbs and spices, with hot dipping sauces or little bowls of fresh, chopped chillies served separately. Palm sugar is used in many dishes and several spices are used which are not normally thought of in the context of oriental food. Cinnamon, turmeric and fennel seeds, for example, are Indian curry spices that reflect south Vietnam's very early history, when Indian trading ships first began to call in on their way to China.

Many centuries later, in the late 1800s, French cuisine began to make its mark on Vietnam, when Vietnam was forced to become a protectorate of France. French bread, made from wheat flour or rice flour, is widely found. A popular street snack is a baguette filled with a Vietnamese version of pâté and salad or pickled vegetables. Of course, the situation has worked both ways, and Paris has been the home of Vietnamese food in Europe for years. It is only recently that other European cities, such as London, have begun to enjoy this cuisine.

After the end of the Vietnam war, in 1973, the north and south of the country were reunited for the first time in over 100 years. During all that time the two regions had lived in extremely different ways, particularly during recent decades with communism in the north, and US-backed capitalism in the south. Many southerners who had worked

for or with the Americans tried desperately to take their families and leave the country altogether. After years of boat people arriving in Hong Kong in ever-increasing numbers, the UN oversaw the legal emigration of hundreds of thousands of Vietnamese to western countries.

A great many Vietnamese went to the west coast of the USA, where they live and prosper in large communities. Among many other things they brought with them, their fish farming skills and their native cuisine are two of the most admired. Much of California's fish and shellfish farming is Vietnamese owned and run. The late 1970s saw the start of Vietnamese restaurants in the USA. Some US servicemen had returned home with a taste for Vietnamese food, and its popularity spread. Today, there are many Vietnamese restaurants, especially on the west coast and in large cities.

Good food and good cooking are important in Vietnam. People eat several times a day, stopping in the street for a bowl of noodle soup or some spring rolls. Noodle soup is eaten at any time of day, from breakfast onwards. There is a vast range of noodle soups – the noodles can be thick or thin; they can be put with pieces of fish, shellfish or fishballs, chicken, beef, or pork balls. The whole lot is put into a large bowl and covered with aromatic stock to which you add your choice of bean sprouts, herbs, chillies, fish sauce, roasted peanuts and lime juice. These soups are healthy and delicious – really a meal in themselves, and they are eaten with chopsticks and a spoon to make it easier.

Rice is central to a Vietnamese meal. Even if noodles are served as well, a meal needs rice. Rice is revered in South-east Asia – so much depends upon whether or not there is a large rice harvest and whether or not the harvest is of good quality. The economies of whole villages, whole areas, depend upon those harvests. In Vietnam, as in Thailand, the informal expression used to announce dinner or to invite a friend to eat with you, literally means 'eat rice'.

Pork is the most common meat in the country. Beef is also eaten,

although a lot of what is called beef is actually buffalo, or sometimes, venison is served. Goats are reared and eaten, but sheep are not. Poultry of all kinds is very popular – chicken, ducks and quails provide eggs as well as meat.

Fish and shellfish are widely eaten: freshwater and sea fish, fresh

and dried. The country is criss-crossed by rivers, tributaries and deltas, and, of course, there is also the sea itself. Even the flooded rice paddies are a source of fish and eels. At the heart of Vietnamese cooking is the ubiquitous Vietnamese fish sauce, *nuoc mam*. This is a very nutritious sauce used as a flavouring during cooking and as the basis of various dipping sauces. It is to be found on every table in the country and is made by straining off the juices from fish that has been fermented in salt for months. Rather like olive oil in Mediterranean countries, the first straining is the best. The second straining is used for cooking rather than in dipping sauces. A very unusual taste to the western palate, it soon becomes almost addictive.

Typically, a family meal will consist of three or four dishes and a large bowl of rice and a dipping sauce, all appearing on the table at the same time. At a formal, celebratory meal, a dozen different dishes or more might be prepared and, again, served simultaneously.

Strong green tea or beer are usually drunk with meals. Although various imported beers are available, there is a good choice of locally produced beers as well. Both tea and coffee are grown in Vietnam and the best quality of both crops is thought to be grown in the central highlands. The Vietnamese take their coffee in very small, strong draughts. It is usually filtered into individual glasses at the table, dripping over condensed milk.

Although a great many salads and vegetables are eaten in Vietnam, it is difficult to be a strict vegetarian. There are a few vegetarian restaurants in the major cities, and there are two or three days each lunar month, the new moon and the full moon, which many Buddhists keep meat-free. The main problem is that many of the vegetables, tofu and vegetable noodle soups will be made with a light chicken stock rather than vegetable stock and, of course, there is the constant use of Vietnamese fish sauce.

The vast majority of Vietnamese people still cook and eat using the simplest utensils. Although bottled gas is now available, many people, particularly in rural parts of the country, still cook over an open fire.

Fortunately for us, we all have rather more modern set-ups in our kitchens, but quite a lot of Vietnamese food lends itself to being cooked on the barbecue and tastes all the more authentic for it.

Most of what you need to cook Vietnamese food will already be in your kitchen, but there are a few things that you may need to acquire. A large wok is really an essential piece of equipment. If you cook on electricity, buy one with a flat base as it can then sit directly on the heat source. A pestle and mortar are important although you can use food processors, large or small, to great effect. The crushing and grinding action that is used with a pestle really releases the juices and fragrance of herbs and spices, and garlic and onions, in a way that a food processor cannot. It is also a really satisfying thing to do. You will also need a steamer of some kind, either a bamboo one from an oriental shop, or a stainless steel one. If you do not own such an item, it is easy to rig one up by using a colander and a lid over a pan of boiling water. Finally, you will need sharp knives and a cleaver. A cleaver can be useful in so many different ways – crushing garlic cloves before you chop them, finely chopping onions and other vegetables and cutting through bones and meat.

You will also need to add a few food items to your store cupboard – Vietnamese fish sauce being an absolute essential. It comes in glass bottles, and, if kept reasonably cool, will keep for years. You might worry if you see crystals at the bottom, especially if it is an old bottle. Don't – fish sauce uses salt in its making, and salt crystals tend to

re-form after a while. You will also need *banh trang*, the Vietnamese version of spring roll wrappers. These are made of rice and are available in packets from oriental shops. They are hard, round and opaque, and soften quite quickly in warm water. Rice noodles, which come in various different shapes and sizes, fresh and dried, are also a must in Vietnamese cooking.

Otherwise, most ingredients are the same herbs and spices you would use when cooking Chinese, Thai and Indian food – lots of garlic, shallots, ginger, galangal, chillies, star anise, cinnamon and turmeric. Palm sugar is worth buying – again, it is something you can easily find in oriental shops. In Vietnam, sugar comes from either palm trees or sugar cane. A classic snack is made of pieces of peeled sugar cane, with prawn paste moulded around the centre of the stick and then grilled.

The Vietnamese use both Indian and Thai curry pastes, oyster sauce and soy sauce, kaffir lime leaves and lots of fresh lemon grass. They pick and mix tastes and ideas from the various countries that surround them, effortlessly incorporating food from totally different cultures that have been influential in Vietnam. But above anything else, they remain distinctly different from and independent of everyone else.

glossary

Aubergine
Asian aubergines are long, thin and pink, small and round or egg shaped, pale green or white. They can also be tiny, round and dark green. They are often available in large supermarkets and Asian and oriental food shops. If you substitute the large purple-black variety more commonly found in the West, remember that they cook faster than the Asian varieties, so adjust your cooking times accordingly.

Bamboo shoots
The young shoots from the base of the bamboo plant, these can be found both fresh and canned in brine. Pale ivory in colour, they have a crisp texture but bland flavour.

Banana leaves
These can be found in Asian and oriental food shops, and are used to contain food during steaming and grilling. You can use aluminium foil or small bowls, depending on your needs, but banana leaves are more authentic and look spectacular. They also impart a faint taste.

Basil
Holy basil is used as commonly as sweet (European) basil in Vietnamese cookery. It has a smaller, darker leaf and attractive purple stalks. It is less sweet than European basil, which may be substituted. Purple basil is also used.

Bean sauce
Black, yellow and red bean sauces made from preserved soya beans are readily available in jars. Black beans are available in cans and bags and should be rinsed and chopped before use.

Unused beans and their liquid can be stored indefinitely if kept in a sealed container in the refrigerator. Beans and bean sauces of all varieties can be bought from most supermarkets and oriental food shops.

Bean sprouts
The young shoots of the mung bean, these have a crisp texture which makes them excellent for salads and stir-fries. Do not store for too long or they will go limp.

Bok choi
Also called pak choi, this is a dark green leafy vegetable with a crunchy white stalk. It can be found in most good supermarkets and is excellent in stir-fries.

Chillies
There are so many different kinds of chilli it would be impossible to list them all. As a general rule, the smaller the chilli the fiercer the heat. Red chillies are slightly less fierce since they become sweeter as they ripen. Most of the heat of chillies is contained in and around the seeds and the inner membrane. Vietnamese cooks often include the seeds, but you may prefer to remove them for a milder flavour. Larger, fresh orange and yellow chillies are often used, for their pretty colours as much as anything else. Occasionally you can buy them from specialist oriental shops and markets, but otherwise use whatever colour you can get. Chillies freeze perfectly. Dried chillies, chilli sauces, chilli pastes and chilli oil are widely available.

Chinese chives
These long, thick chives are altogether more substantial in appearance than English chives

and have a much stronger flavour. They are sold in oriental shops where you should look for ones with shiny green stems which snap crisply.

Coconut milk and cream
These are widely available in cans, packets and blocks (which require water added). You can make coconut milk yourself from desiccated coconut: place 175 g (6 oz) coconut in a blender with 300 ml (½ pint) hand-hot water; blend for 30 seconds, then strain the liquid through muslin, squeezing it as dry as you can. This will produce thick coconut milk. If you return the coconut to the blender and repeat the process, then mix the two extractions, you will get a medium-thick coconut milk, suitable for most dishes. If you put this milk in the refrigerator the 'cream' will rise to the surface and can be taken off. Coconut milk lasts only 1–2 days, even in the refrigerator. If you are using coconut cream, stir it all the time while cooking because it curdles easily.

Coriander
An essential ingredient. All of this herb is used – the leaves, stalks and roots. You can store the roots in an airtight container in the refrigerator or in the freezer.

Curry paste
Ready-made Indian and Thai curry pastes are widely available.

Fish sauce
Nuoc mam is essential to Vietnamese cooking. It is on every table in Vietnam, and in every kitchen. It is different from Thai fish sauce in the same way that Japanese soy sauces are different from Chinese. It is made from tiny fish that are layered with salt and left to ferment in large earthernware vats for some months.

Five spice powder
An exotic mixture of spices, including Chinese cinnamon, cloves and fennel.

Galangal
Vietnamese cooks use galangal a great deal. It is from the same family as ginger, but the skin is thinner and slightly pink, and the taste is more earthy and mellow. It is sometimes available in large supermarkets and oriental food shops. Use ginger if you cannot find it. Galangal is peeled before use, then sliced or chopped according to individual recipes. Sliced or chopped galangal can be kept in an airtight container in the refrigerator for up to 2 weeks; it also freezes well. Dried slices are also available, and 1 dried slice is the equivalent of 1 cm (½ inch) of the fresh root. Powdered galangal can also be found, but it is not so good.

Ginger
Fresh root ginger is readily available. Use it in the same way as galangal, above.

Glutinous rice
A variety of short-grain rice used in many Vietnamese desserts. Sometimes called 'sticky' rice, it is also used with savoury dishes. For example, it is combined with chicken or pork and spices, wrapped in a banana leaf and steamed.

Kaffir limes and lime leaves
These are slightly different from the ones we normally see, which make a perfectly adequate substitute. Kaffir lime leaves can be bought fresh or dried in oriental food shops and large supermarkets; they freeze perfectly. If unavailable use lime rind or juice, or lemon rind or juice as a last resort.

Lemon grass
Available from supermarkets in

bundles of 4–6 stalks, the straw-like tops should be trimmed as well as the ends, and the stalks thinly sliced. If you can't get fresh lemon grass, dried and powdered lemon grass is also available, or you can use lemon rind or juice as a substitute.

Lily bulbs and buds

These are available from oriental shops, dried. The bulbs need soaking in hot water before use; the buds are usually cooked in slow-cooked dishes. They have a unique flavour.

Mint

There are many different types of fresh mint available in Vietnam and they are used almost all the time as a garnish or wrapped up with grilled meat or fish in lettuce leaves or spring rolls.

Mushrooms

DRIED BLACK FUNGUS (cloud ear mushrooms) can be found in packets in oriental food shops. They should be soaked in warm water for 15–20 minutes, then washed and drained and any hard pieces removed before they are cooked.

OYSTER MUSHROOMS are available fresh from most supermarkets. SHIITAKE MUSHROOMS can be found dried in oriental food shops, health food shops and some supermarkets, which also sell them fresh occasionally. If dried, they should be soaked in warm water for 15–20 minutes before use, then the hard stalk cut away and added to the stockpot. Shiitake are expensive, but you only need to use a few at a time. STRAW MUSHROOMS can be found in cans from supermarkets.

Noodles

There are many different kinds of noodles used in Vietnamese cooking, but those most commonly available are fresh or dried rice sticks, rice vermicelli

and glass noodles. Egg noodles are used, but less frequently than rice noodles.

RICE STICKS are the same as vermicelli, only wider and flatter. They come in varying widths, and it is a matter of personal preference which ones you choose. Fresh rice sticks can be found in oriental shops; these are white and slippery and can be cut to any desired width. They do not keep well, and so should be used on the day of purchase.

RICE VERMICELLI are very thin, white and transparent-looking, made from rice as their name suggests. They are dried in long bundles, but can be cut into more convenient lengths with scissors. GLASS NOODLES are also known as cellophane noodles, bean thread noodles and bean vermicelli. They are very like rice vermicelli, but made from mung beans rather than rice.

EGG NOODLES can be bought fresh from oriental shops, but the dried ones, which are available at supermarkets, are just as good.

Oil

Groundnut oil is commonly used in South-east Asia because so many peanuts are grown and used, although other vegetable oils can be used. Do not use olive oil because the taste is too distinctive. After using oil for deep-frying, let it cool, then strain it through a fine sieve or muslin back into the bottle for future use. You can then keep this oil specially for oriental cooking.

Palm sugar

This soft, raw light brown sugar is widely used in South-east Asia. In Thailand, it is often sold wet, giving it a thick, honey-like consistency, but it is exported in hard blocks that can be broken into pieces and dissolved. It tastes delicious and has a golden colour that is especially attractive in desserts such as coconut

custard. If you can't get it, use golden granulated, a light muscovado or Indian jaggery.

Papaya

Also called pawpaw, this tropical fruit is available from supermarkets. When unripe, the pale green flesh is used in salads. The hard orange flesh of most supermarket papayas can be used the same way. The soft orange flesh of ripe papaya tastes best with a little lime juice.

Rice paper wrappers

Banh trang are made of rice flour, water and salt. They come in square or round shapes and are hard and opaque. They have to be soaked in water and are then used either as deep-fried spring rolls or rolled up around salad and cold fish or meat.

Soy sauce

Light soy sauce is a thin, savoury liquid made from fermented soya beans. It is used extensively in oriental cookery. Dark soy sauce is not only darker in colour, but it is also thicker and sweeter.

Star anise

The small, dried, star-shaped fruit of an evergreen tree that is cultivated only in China and parts of South-east Asia; it tastes of aniseed.

Tamarind water

Dried tamarind pulp can be found in oriental and Indian food shops. Simmer for 2–3 minutes, allow to cool, then squeeze out the juice and discard the pulp and seeds. Tamarind concentrate can be bought in tubs – just dissolve a spoonful in hot water. You can substitute lemon juice.

Tofu

Made from soya beans, tofu is highly nutritious and absorbs other flavours, making it a versatile addition to a vegetarian

diet. There are several kinds of tofu available. Fresh white tofu is sold in blocks in its own liquid. It is very delicate and will break up if stirred too much. It does not keep long. Blocks of ready-fried tofu are golden brown on the outside and much more solid. They are ideal for stir-frying. You can buy fairly solid white tofu cakes packed in water in plastic containers; these can be used for stir-frying if you can't get the ready-fried kind. Sheets of tofu, sometimes called 'bean-curd skins', are made from heated soya milk. They are dried, and need to be soaked for 2–3 hours before use. These products are available in health food shops, supermarkets and oriental stores.

Turmeric

This spice is a wonderful colourant with a mild flavour. Although it can sometimes be found fresh in oriental and Asian food shops, it is most often used in its powdered form.

Vinegar

It is worth looking for white and red rice vinegar or distilled white vinegar in large supermarkets or oriental shops. If you cannot find them, use cider vinegar. Malt vinegar will not suit oriental food.

Water chestnuts

Despite their name, these are not chestnuts but tubers that grow in paddy fields and are sold fresh and in cans. Although they have a bland taste, their crisp texture makes them an excellent addition to stir-fries.

Wonton wrappers

Made from flour and eggs, these are yellow or brown in colour. They are sold ready-made, fresh or frozen in bags, from oriental food shops. If a recipe uses shaped wrappers, cut them to shape. Otherwise, use sheets of filo pastry and cut them to size.

soups

In Vietnam, as in most Asian countries, a meal will consist of an assortment of different dishes. Typically, this means a large bowl of rice, a fish or meat dish, vegetables, often in the form of a salad plate, and soup. Many people will not drink anything, even water, while they eat, so a soup supplies the liquid element. Most meals are rounded off with a glass of green tea, which acts as a digestive. The soups in this chapter range from Prawn & Watercress Soup (see page 16), which would make an excellent dinner party starter, to the substantial and filling Stuffed Cabbage Soup (see page 20).

prawn & lemon grass soup

sup tom xoa lan

375 g (12 oz) raw prawns

3 lemon grass stalks

1.2 litres (2 pints) water

1 tomato, quartered and deseeded

475 g (15 oz) can straw mushrooms drained

6 kaffir lime leaves

1 spring onion

185 g (6½ oz) bean sprouts

juice of 3 limes

2 small red chillies, finely sliced

4 tablespoons Vietnamese fish sauce

salt and pepper

coriander leaves, to garnish

This dish can become a light main course if you serve it with rice.

1 Peel and devein the prawns and set aside the shells. Cut off the white part of the lemon grass stalks, reserving the tops. Cut the lemon grass stalks into 2.5 cm (1 inch) lengths and flatten with a cleaver or pestle.

2 Heat the water in a saucepan, add the prawn shells and the lemon grass tops. Bring the water slowly to the boil, strain and return to the saucepan. Add the flattened lemon grass, tomato, straw mushrooms and lime leaves. Bring back to the boil then reduce the heat to a simmer and cook for 3–4 minutes.

3 Add the prawns and when they have changed colour, add the spring onion, bean sprouts, lime juice, chillies, fish sauce and season to taste with salt and pepper, then give it all a good stir.

4 Serve in individual bowls, sprinkled with coriander leaves.

Serves 4

prawn & watercress soup

canh sa lach soan

1.2 litres (2 pints) Fish Stock (see page 134) or Vegetable Stock (see page 135)

125 g (4 oz) raw prawns

1 small shallot, finely chopped

2½ tablespoons Vietnamese fish sauce

pinch of pepper

leaves from 1 bunch of watercress

1 Pour the stock into a large saucepan and bring gently to the boil.

2 Meanwhile peel the prawns, devein them and set aside the shells. Pound the shallot in a mortar and add the prawns, fish sauce and pepper. Pound again to ensure the prawns absorb the other flavours.

3 When the stock is boiling, add the prawn shells and simmer for 5 minutes. Remove and discard the shells, then add the prawn mixture. After about 1 minute, when the prawns have changed colour, add the watercress. Simmer for 1 more minute and serve.

Serves 4

chicken & pumpkin soup

canh ga bi doa

1 Pour the stock into a saucepan and bring to the boil. Add the chicken thighs and simmer for 10–15 minutes, until cooked through. Remove and set aside.

2 Add the pumpkin cubes to the stock with the spring onions, fish sauce and pepper. While the pumpkin is simmering, strip the meat from the chicken and return it to the pan. Serve the soup garnished with coriander leaves.

Serves 4

1.2 litres (2 pints) Chicken Stock (see page 134)

2 chicken thighs

450 g (14½ oz) pumpkin, peeled and cut into 1 cm (½ inch) cubes

2 spring onions, sliced

2 tablespoons Vietnamese fish sauce

1 teaspoon pepper

coriander leaves, to garnish

pork ball & tofu soup

sup lon tau pho

1 Put the pork, pepper, garlic, shallot, chilli and fish sauce into a small food processor and process until smooth, then form the mixture into 8 small balls.

2 Bring the stock to a simmer, add the meatballs and cook for about 8 minutes. Add the bok choi and cook for another 3–4 minutes. Add the tofu cubes and warm through. Serve the soup garnished with coriander sprigs.

Serves 4

125 g (4 oz) lean pork, chopped

½ teaspoon pepper

1 large garlic clove, crushed and finely chopped

½ tablespoon finely chopped shallot

½ small red chilli, finely chopped

1 tablespoon Vietnamese fish sauce

1 litre (1¾ pints) Vegetable Stock (see page 135) or Chicken Stock (see page 134)

1 head (125 g/4 oz) bok choi, finely sliced

1 block firm tofu, cubed

coriander sprigs, to garnish

crab & asparagus soup

sup mang tay cua

Asparagus is readily available in Vietnam – it was introduced by the French and is grown in the Da Lat area.

1 Pour the stock into a saucepan and bring to a simmer.

2 Cut the tips from the asparagus and set aside. Cut the stalks into 2.5 cm (1 inch) pieces, add them to the stock and simmer until they are soft. Add the mushroom soaking liquid.

3 Mix the cornflour with the water and add to the stock, stirring to thicken. Pour in the beaten egg, using a fork to stir the stock as you pour, then add the asparagus tips and the mushrooms. Simmer for about 4 minutes – the asparagus tips should still have some bite.

4 Finally, add the crab meat, season to taste with salt and pepper and warm it through. Serve in warmed individual bowls.

Serves 4

1 litre (1¾ pints) Vegetable Stock (see page 135)

250 g (8 oz) asparagus spears

4 dried shiitake mushrooms, soaked and sliced, soaking liquid reserved

1 tablespoon cornflour

1 tablespoon cold water

1 egg, beaten

250 g (8 oz) white crab meat

salt and pepper

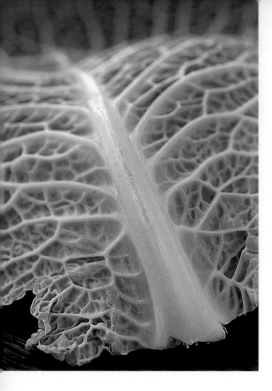

stuffed cabbage soup

sup cai bap

1 Cook the cabbage leaves in lightly salted boiling water for about 2 minutes, until softened. Drain and set aside.

2 Put the spring onions, black fungus and pork into a small food processor with the pepper and ½ tablespoon Vietnamese fish sauce and process until smooth.

3 Pour the stock into a saucepan and heat to a simmer. While it is heating, make the cabbage rolls. Place a teaspoon of filling on each leaf, fold in the sides and roll them up from the bottom. You will make 16–20 rolls. Secure them with cocktail sticks and add them to the stock with the remaining fish sauce. Cover the pan and simmer for 10–12 minutes.

Serves 4

12 tender Savoy cabbage leaves, halved lengthways and central rib removed

100 g (3½ oz) spring onion whites, finely chopped

4 dried black fungus, soaked and shredded

125 g (4 oz) minced pork

½ teaspoon pepper

2½ tablespoons Vietnamese fish sauce

1.2 litres (2 pints) Chicken Stock (see page 134)

salt

starters

Starters are not really part of the Vietnamese way of life. The scrumptious snacks in this chapter are commonly available throughout the day on every street corner. People stop when they are hungry or when they see and smell something irresistible. They will sit down on a small stool or bench, by a rickety table set up on the pavement, and wait for their sizzling pancake or whatever it is to be cooked for them. These dishes would normally appear in the Vietnamese homc only as part of a large, formal dinner. However, they are just the thing when you want new ideas for party nibbles, picnics or barbecue food or just a late night snack.

stuffed pancakes

bahn xeo

1 Whisk the flour and water together thoroughly in a bowl and leave to stand while you prepare the filling.

2 Heat the vegetable oil in a wok and stir-fry the prawns, pork, shallot and bean sprouts for 3 minutes until cooked.

3 Brush a 20 cm (8 inch) frying pan with a little oil and place over a high heat. Pour in enough batter to cover the bottom of the pan and tip any excess back into the bowl. Spread a thin layer of filling on to one half of the pancake, fold the other half over it and cook for about 4 minutes, until the bottom is crisp. Turn the pancake over and continue to cook for another minute or two, then remove to a plate. Continue until you have made all 8 pancakes.

4 To serve, cut the pancakes into pieces and wrap each piece inside a lettuce leaf with the cucmber and a few herbs. Eat with nuoc cham dipping sauce.

Makes 8

250 g (8 oz) rice flour

375 ml (13 fl oz) water

1 tablespoon vegetable oil, plus extra for cooking the pancakes

125 g (4 oz) raw prawns, peeled and deveined

100 g (3½ oz) pork fillet, minced

1 shallot, finely chopped

125 g (4 oz) bean sprouts

To serve:

lettuce leaves

1 cucumber, deseeded and grated

dill, mint and coriander leaves

Nuoc Cham Dipping Sauce (see page 141)

eel cakes

cha luon

Ask your fishmonger to skin, bone and chop the eel for you.

500 g (1 lb) eel, skinned, boned and chopped

250 g (8 oz) cod fillet, chopped

2 lemon grass stalks, finely chopped

4 shallots, finely chopped

2 garlic cloves, finely chopped

1 small red chilli, finely chopped

1 teaspoon Vietnamese fish sauce

½ teaspoon golden caster sugar

salt and pepper

vegetable oil, for frying

To serve:

crisp lettuce leaves

coriander, dill and mint leaves

Nuoc Cham Dipping Sauce (see page 141)

1 Put all the ingredients, except the oil, into a food processor with a pinch of salt and pepper and process to a paste. Turn the paste into a bowl, cover and chill in the refrigerator for 1 hour, then form into 16 cakes.

2 Heat the oil in a frying pan and gently fry the eel cakes for 3–4 minutes on each side, until golden brown.

3 To serve, let each guest wrap up an eel cake in a lettuce leaf with a handful of herbs, and dip the parcel into the dipping sauce.

Makes 16

prawn & sweet potato cakes

khoai lang chien voi tom

1 Cut the sweet potatoes into long thin sticks – this is easily done on a mandoline – and toss them with about two-thirds of the flour. Cover the prawns with the remaining flour.

2 Heat 5 mm (¼ inch) of oil in a large frying pan and, when it is hot, put in 4 egg poaching rings. Fill them about half full with the sweet potato, pushing it down. Place a prawn on top. After 1½ minutes, carefully remove the poaching rings, but do not disturb the sweet potato cakes at all. When they have cooked for about 4 minutes the bottoms will be golden brown and crispy. Carefully flip them over and cook them on the other side for another 2 minutes. Watch the heat – you do not want them to burn, but they will not stick together if the heat is too low. Drain on kitchen paper and keep warm while cooking the remainder. Serve with lime wedges.

Makes 12

375 g (12 oz) sweet potatoes, peeled

75 g (3 oz) flour

12 raw medium prawns, peeled and deveined

vegetable oil, for frying

lime wedges, to garnish

crystal prawn rolls

tom tai chanh

1 Put the vinegar and salt into a bowl and stir in the prawns. Leave for about 7 minutes, then drain the prawns, rinse well under running water and squeeze them dry. They will look whiteish and not very attractive.

2 Put the shallot, garlic, chillies, fish sauce and lime juice into another bowl, add the prawns and mix thoroughly. Cover and leave to marinate in the refrigerator for about 3–4 hours, until the prawns have changed colour.

3 Soak the rice paper wrappers in hot water, one at a time, until they become soft and flexible, then remove them and pat dry.

4 Put some of the prawn mixture in a line, about 2.5 cm (1 inch) from the edge of the wrapper, add some peanuts and mixed herbs and roll up the wrapper, folding in the sides to make a neat cigar shape. As these rice paper wrappers are usually quite large, cut the prawn rolls into halves or thirds. Serve with individual bowls of nuoc cham dipping sauce.

Makes 8

125 ml (4 fl oz) white rice vinegar

pinch of salt

500 g (1 lb) medium raw prawns, peeled, deveined and halved lengthways

1 shallot, finely chopped

2 garlic cloves, finely chopped

2 small green chillies, finely chopped

1½ tablespoons Vietnamese fish sauce

juice of 1–2 limes

8 round rice paper wrappers

60 g (2½ oz) Crushed Roasted Peanuts (see page 141)

large handful of coriander, dill and mint leaves

Nuoc Cham Dipping Sauce (see page 141), to serve

pork & crab spring rolls

cha gio

These spring rolls take a while to make, but they are well worth it. You can make them a day or two in advance and fry them lightly until they are a pale gold colour, then keep them covered in the refrigerator. Just before you need them, fry them again to a golden brown. Serve with nuoc cham dipping sauce or sweet chilli sauce.

1 In a large bowl, mix together the vermicelli, black fungus, pork, crab meat, shallot, garlic, salt, pepper and 1 of the eggs. Beat the remaining eggs well in another bowl.

2 Using a pastry brush, coat both sides of each rice paper wrapper with beaten egg. Do this one at a time and quite quickly, at the same time as you fill them, as they can be tricky to get off the work surface if you leave them too long. Put a spoonful of filling on each wrapper, shape it like a cigar so that it comes to within 2.5 cm (1 inch) of each side, then roll it up, folding in the sides neatly. When all the spring rolls are done, deep-fry them for about 5 minutes at 190°C (375°F) until golden brown and crispy. Serve with the nuoc cham dipping sauce or quick sweet chilli sauce.

Makes 8–12

25 g (1 oz) rice vermicelli, soaked and cut into 2.5 cm (1 inch) lengths

2 tablespoons dried black fungus, soaked and chopped

375 g (12 oz) lean minced pork

100 g (3½ oz) crab meat

1 shallot, finely chopped

1 large garlic clove, finely chopped

½ teaspoon salt

1 teaspoon pepper

3 eggs

8–12 round rice paper wrappers

vegetable oil, for deep-frying

Nuoc Cham Dipping Sauce (see page 141) or Quick Sweet Chilli Sauce (see page 142), to serve

vietnamese dumplings

banh cuon

1 Mix the pork, black fungus, shallots, garlic, chilli, coriander, salt and pepper in a bowl.

2 Heat the oil in a wok and stir-fry the pork mixture for about 5 minutes, or until cooked through. Allow to cool.

3 Mix together the cornflour and water in a bowl, adding a little more water if needed.

4 With your finger, paint some of the cornflour mixture around the edge of a wonton wrapper. Put a teaspoonful of the pork mixture on the wrapper in a sausage shape. Roll up the wrapper, pressing the edges together. Continue until all the filling is used up.

5 Steam or gently boil the dumplings for 5–6 minutes and then serve, garnished with the shallots and cucumber sticks, and with the dipping sauce.

Makes 20–24

500 g (1 lb) lean pork, minced

2 tablespoons dried black fungus, soaked and finely chopped

2 small shallots, finely chopped

2 garlic cloves, finely minced

1 green chilli, finely minced

25 g (1 oz) coriander leaves and stalks

1 teaspoon salt

1 teaspoon pepper

2 tablespoons vegetable oil

1 tablespoon cornflour

2 tablespoons water

20–24 wonton wrappers

Nuoc Cham Dipping Sauce (see page 141), to serve

To garnish:

Crispy Fried Shallots (see page 139)

cucumber sticks

crab cakes

cha cua

450 g (14½ oz) mixed white and brown crab meat

2 small shallots, finely minced

1 garlic clove, finely minced

1 tablespoon chopped coriander

1 tablespoon Vietnamese fish sauce

½ teaspoon pepper

½ egg, beaten

breadcrumbs (optional)

vegetable oil, for frying

Chinese chive flowers, to garnish

To serve:

Salad Plate (see page 56)

Nuoc Cham Dipping Sauce (see page 141)

Try to use fresh crab meat for this dish – the frozen sort is always very wet and quite often fairly tasteless.

1 Put the crab meat, shallots, garlic, coriander, fish sauce, pepper and egg into a bowl and mix together, then form into 12–16 cakes. If the crab meat was frozen and the mixture is too sloppy, add some breadcrumbs to stiffen the mixture a little. Place the cakes on a plate and chill in the refrigerator for about 1 hour to firm up.

2 Heat about 5 mm (¼ inch) of oil in a large frying pan and add the crab cakes. Cook without moving them for 2–3 minutes, until brown and crusty underneath. Turn them over carefully and cook for another 2–3 minutes, then remove and drain on kitchen paper. Serve the crab cakes garnished with Chinese chive flowers and with the salad and nuoc cham dipping sauce.

Makes 12–16

stuffed scallops

so nuong don cha rau

20 small cooked peeled prawns, finely chopped

1 piece dried black fungus, soaked and finely chopped

125 g (4 oz) sweet potato, boiled and mashed

1 tablespoon Vietnamese fish sauce

12 live king scallops, on the shell

salt and pepper

coriander sprigs, to garnish

Nuoc Cham Dipping Sauce (see page 141), to serve

1 Mix the prawns, black fungus, sweet potato and fish sauce and season with salt and pepper. Carefully make a horizontal slit in each scallop and spoon in some of the stuffing.

2 Steam the scallops, in their shells, for about 5 minutes. You should be able to cook them in 2 batches. Garnish with coriander sprigs and serve with nuoc cham dipping sauce.

Serves 4

crab omelette

trung chien voi cua

5 large eggs

1½ tablespoons vegetable oil

1 small shallot, finely chopped

1 small red chilli, finely sliced

150 g (5 oz) crab meat

splash of Vietnamese fish sauce

salt and pepper

coriander sprigs, to garnish

Nuoc Cham Dipping Sauce (see page 141), to serve.

1 Beat the eggs in a bowl with a pinch of salt and pepper.

2 Heat 1 tablespoon of the oil in a wok and fry the shallot and chilli for 1 minute. Add the crab meat to the wok and continue to stir and fry for 1 more minute. Splash in a little fish sauce and mix it in. Move the crab mixture to one side of the wok.

3 Heat the remaining oil in the wok. Pour in the eggs, swirl them around and make a thinnish omelette. When the bottom is set but the top is still creamy, add the crab mixture to one side of the omelette, folding the other side over it. Serve immediately, garnished with coriander sprigs, with the dipping sauce.

Serves 2

prawn toast

banh mi chien voi tom

1 Mix together the prawns, pork, sugar, shallot, garlic, fish sauce, ginger and egg and spread the mixture on the bread. Press some sesame seeds on to each piece.

2 Heat the oil in a large wok and slide the bread into it, 2 pieces at a time, spread side up. Deep-fry for about 4–5 minutes, until golden. Turn each slice over and fry for 30 seconds, then remove from the wok and drain on kitchen paper.

3 Cut each piece of bread into halves or quarters, garnish with basil sprigs and serve with nuoc cham dipping sauce.

Makes 16–32

185 g (6½ oz) raw prawns, peeled, deveined and finely chopped

125 g (4 oz) lean pork, finely minced

1 teaspoon palm sugar

1 shallot, finely chopped

2 large garlic cloves, crushed and finely chopped

1 tablespoon Vietnamese fish sauce

½ teaspoon finely chopped ginger

1 large egg

8 slices of bread

2 teaspoons sesame seeds

vegetable oil, for deep-frying

basil sprigs, to garnish

Nuoc Cham Dipping Sauce (see page 141), to serve

stuffed chicken wings

canh ga nhoi thit

12 large chicken wings

15 g (½ oz) rice vermicelli

1 tablespoon groundnut oil

½ spring onion

2 garlic cloves, crushed and
finely chopped

1 tablespoon finely chopped
lemon grass

1 tablespoon Vietnamese fish sauce

50 g (2 oz) pork, finely minced

100 g (3½ oz) water chestnuts,
chopped

1 tablespoon finely chopped
coriander leaves

2 dried black fungus, softened in
hot water and finely chopped

125 g (4 oz) raw prawns, peeled,
deveined and finely chopped

vegetable oil, for deep-frying

mint sprigs, to garnish

Nuoc Cham Dipping Sauce (see
page 141), to serve

1 Cut the thick sections from the chicken wings, leaving the middle section and wingtip whole. To bone the wings, twist the middle joint to break it. Then, holding the bone in your left hand, carefully scrape the meat away from it, without breaking the skin, and pull out the bones. This is easier than it sounds but it is time consuming. If you have a good butcher and give him some notice, he will be able to do it for you.

2 Cook the vermicelli in lightly salted boiling water, then rinse under cold water. Cut the strands into 2.5 cm (1 inch) lengths and set aside.

3 Heat the oil in a wok and stir-fry the spring onion, garlic, lemon grass, fish sauce, pork, water chestnuts, coriander leaves and black fungus for 4 minutes, or until the pork is cooked. Add the prawns and stir-fry until they turn pink – about 1 minute. Remove the wok from the heat, stir in the vermicelli and allow the mixture to cool.

4 Fill the boned chicken wings with the mixture, leaving a little space at the top to allow for shrinkage. Use cocktail sticks to close the tops. Heat the oil in a deep-fryer to very hot and deep-fry the wings, in batches, for about 10 minutes, until lightly browned and cooked through. Remove carefully from the deep-fryer and drain on kitchen paper. Serve with nuoc cham dipping sauce and garnish with mint sprigs.

Serves 4

chicken parcels

ga cuon

1 Combine the lime juice, fish sauce, honey and cornflour in a bowl and set aside.

2 Heat the oil in a wok and stir-fry the garlic, spring onions and chillies for 1 minute. Add the chicken, water chestnuts and mushrooms and stir-fry for 2–3 minutes, until the chicken is cooked through. Stir the sauce in the bowl and add it to the wok with the bean sprouts and season to taste with salt and pepper. Stir-fry for 1 minute, then add the peanuts and mint.

3 To serve, turn all the mixture out on to the centre of a warmed platter and arrange the lettuce leaves around it. To eat it, place some of the chicken mixture on a lettuce leaf, fold it up, and dip it into the sauce.

Serves 4

juice of 1½ limes

2 tablespoons Vietnamese fish sauce

4 teaspoons clear honey

2 teaspoons cornflour

1 tablespoon vegetable oil

2 large garlic cloves, finely minced

2 spring onions, finely minced

2 small red chillies, finely sliced

250 g (8 oz) boneless, skinless chicken breast, finely chopped

125 g (4 oz) water chestnuts, chopped

6 shiitake mushrooms, soaked and finely chopped

125 g (4 oz) bean sprouts

2 tablespoons Crushed Roasted Peanuts (see page 141)

2 tablespoons chopped mint leaves

salt and pepper

To serve:

lettuce leaves

Nuoc Cham Dipping Sauce (see page 141)

vegetarian crystal rolls

bi cuon chay viet nam

These are lovely, clean-tasting rolls, very good for serving as a snack in the summertime.

1 Soak a rice paper wrapper in warm water for 1–2 minutes, until soft. Carefully remove it to a board. Place a little of all the ingredients on the wrapper, in a cigar shape, making sure you leave enough room at the sides to fold them in. Roll up the wrapper neatly, set aside, and continue with the remaining wrappers and filling. Serve with the dipping sauce.

Makes 8

8 rice paper wrappers

50 g (2 oz) rice vermicelli, soaked and cut into 2.5 cm (1 inch) lengths

8 small asparagus spears, cooked and cooled

6 shiitake mushrooms, soaked and cut into shreds

½ cucumber, peeled, deseeded and grated

50 g (2 oz) bamboo shoots, chopped

60 g (2½ oz) bean sprouts, blanched

1 carrot, grated

2 tablespoons Crushed Roasted Peanuts (see page 141)

coriander, basil, mint and chive leaves

Nuoc Cham Dipping Sauce (see page 141), to serve

vietnamese satay

nem nuong

1 Mix together the pork, garlic, sugar, salt, pepper, rice wine and groundnut oil in a bowl, cover and leave to marinate overnight.

2 Thread the pork cubes on to pre-soaked bamboo skewers and cook under a preheated grill for about 10 minutes, turning frequently.

3 To eat the pork, wrap a piece in a noodle cake with some fresh herbs or a piece of lettuce. Pull the pork from the skewer, and dip it into the peanut sauce or dipping sauce.

Makes 4

500 g (1 lb) slightly fatty pork, cut into 1 cm (½ inch) cubes

4 garlic cloves, crushed and chopped

1 dessertspoon palm sugar

½ teaspoon salt

½ teaspoon pepper

2 tablespoons Chinese rice wine

1 tablespoon groundnut oil

To serve:

Noodle Cakes (see page 51)

Salad Plate (see page 56)

Easy Peanut Sauce (see page 143)

Nuoc Cham Dipping Sauce (see page 141)

grilled beef in vine leaves

bo la lot

250 g (8 oz) rump steak, finely chopped

60 g (2½ oz) pork fat, finely chopped

2 lemon grass stalks, finely chopped

1 large garlic clove, finely chopped

1 teaspoon ground turmeric

1 teaspoon ground cinnamon

2 teaspoons five spice powder

1 teaspoon palm or golden caster sugar

1 teaspoon salt

1 teaspoon pepper

16 vine leaves, thoroughly washed if packed in brine

vegetable oil, for brushing

Nuoc Cham Dipping Sauce (see page 141), to serve

In Vietnam, these delicious little beef snacks are actually rolled in La Lot leaves; these are very hard to find but vine leaves make a sensible alternative. They are lovely cooked on the barbecue.

1 Mix together the steak, pork fat, lemon grass, garlic, turmeric, cinnamon, five spice powder, sugar, salt and pepper in a large bowl, cover and leave to marinate for several hours or overnight in the refrigerator.

2 Place a vine leaf flat on a board and put a heaped teaspoon of filling about one-third of the way up. Fold the sides over and then roll up the leaf neatly from the bottom. Repeat with the remaining vine leaves and filling.

3 When you have stuffed all the vine leaves, brush them with a little oil and grill them under a preheated grill for about 10 minutes, turning from time to time. Serve with the dipping sauce.

Makes 16

rice & noodles

Rice is the staple food of Vietnam and is served at every meal, even when noodles are also available. The most notable exception to this rule is noodle soups, of which there are various types. These consist of a variety of spices and vegetables together with a few pieces of beef, chicken, prawns or fishballs, all arranged on a bed of rice noodles, covered with a tasty stock and garnished with fresh herbs, crushed roasted peanuts and crispy fried shallots. Noodle soup makes an excellent breakfast. It also makes an excellent midday meal or late-night supper. Luckily it is very widely available in Vietnam.

chicken noodle soup

pho ga

1.2 litres (2 pints) Chicken Stock
(see page 134)

1 tablespoon Vietnamese fish sauce

60 g (2½ oz) galangal, finely chopped

2 star anise

2 cinnamon sticks

1 teaspoon sugar

250 g (8 oz) boneless, skinless
chicken

250 g (8 oz) rice noodles

4 spring onions, diagonally sliced

250 g (8 oz) bean sprouts

4 small red chillies, finely chopped

2 limes, quartered

Crispy Fried Shallots (see page 139)

Crushed Roasted Peanuts
(see page 141)

handful of coriander leaves

salt and pepper

It is important to use a good quality chicken stock for this recipe.

1 Pour the stock into a large saucepan and add the fish sauce, galangal, star anise, cinnamon, sugar and season to taste with salt and pepper. Simmer for 10 minutes, add the chicken and simmer for a further 10–15 minutes, then remove the chicken to a plate, shred it and place the shreds in a bowl.

2 Cook the rice noodles according to the packet instructions and divide them between 4 large bowls. Divide the chicken shreds between the bowls and pour over the strained chicken soup.

3 Place all the remaining ingredients on the table in small bowls so that everyone can help themselves.

Serves 4

saigon noodles

pho saigon

4 tablespoons light soy sauce

2 tablespoons oyster sauce

1 tablespoon Vietnamese fish sauce

juice of 1 lime

250 g (8 oz) boneless, skinless
chicken, cut into bite-sized pieces

150 g (5 oz) pork fillet, thinly sliced

300 g (10 oz) raw prawns, peeled,
deveined and halved lengthways

375 g (12 oz) thick rice noodles

2 tablespoons groundnut oil

6 garlic cloves, crushed
and chopped

2 shallots, finely chopped

200 g (7 oz) bok choi, shredded

25 g (1 oz) bamboo shoots

handful of bean sprouts

6 asparagus spears, cooked and
chopped into 5 cm (2 inch) lengths

coriander leaves, to garnish

1 Mix the soy, oyster and fish sauces with the lime juice and divide them between 2 bowls. Put the chicken and pork in one and the prawns in the other and leave to marinate for an hour.

2 Cook the rice noodles according to the packet instructions and set aside in a colander.

3 Heat the oil in a large wok and stir-fry the garlic and shallots for 30 seconds. Add the chicken and pork with their marinade. Stir and fry until the meats change colour, then add the bok choi, bamboo shoots, bean sprouts, prawns and asparagus. Stir and toss until the prawns change colour. Finally, run warm water through the cooked noodles and separate them then add them to the wok. Stir and fry everything together, adding a little water if the mixture seems too dry. Serve garnished with coriander leaves.

Serves 4

prawn fried rice

com huong giang

2 tablespoons vegetable oil

2 garlic cloves, finely minced

3 shallots, finely minced

2 lemon grass stalks,
finely chopped

1 small red chilli, finely sliced

green leaves of 2 spring
onions, sliced

250 g (8 oz) raw prawns, peeled,
deveined and chopped

500 g (1 lb) cooked Thai jasmine
rice, cooled

2 tablespoons coriander
leaves, chopped

salt and pepper

1 Heat the oil in a wok, add the garlic, shallots, lemon grass and chilli and stir-fry over a high heat for 1 minute. Add the spring onions and prawns and stir-fry briefly until the prawns have changed colour. Add the rice and coriander leaves, season to taste with salt and pepper and stir-fry until heated through.

Serves 4

beef noodle soup

pho bo

1 Put the bones, beef, water, ginger, shallots, star anise, cinnamon, tangerine peel, if using, and fish sauce into a large saucepan or casserole and season to taste with salt and pepper. Bring to the boil, skimming. Reduce the heat to simmering point and cook for about 2½ hours, skimming when necessary. Strain the soup, remove the pieces of beef and cut them up.

2 Put the fresh noodles into a pan of boiling water and heat through, then drain. Divide the noodles and meat between 4 bowls and pour the soup over them. Garnish each bowl with coriander sprigs. Put the bean sprouts, chillies, lime wedges, spring onions and fish sauce in separate dishes and let people help themselves.

Serves 4

750 g (1½ lb) beef bones

500 g (1 lb) braising steak, cut into large pieces

2.5 litres (4 pints) water

2.5 cm (1 inch) piece fresh root ginger, peeled and sliced

4 large shallots, thinly sliced

3 star anise

1 cinnamon stick

2 pieces dried tangerine peel (optional)

2 tablespoons Vietnamese fish sauce

500 g (1 lb) fresh flat rice noodles

salt and pepper

coriander sprigs, to garnish

To serve:

bean sprouts

chopped red chillies

lime wedges

sliced spring onions

Vietnamese fish sauce

crab with rice noodles

cua xao bun tau

1 Cook the rice vermicelli according to packet instructions and set aside.

2 Heat the oil in a wok and fry the shallots for 1 minute, then add the garlic and stir-fry for another 30 seconds. Add the crab and cook, stirring, for 2 minutes, then add the water, fish sauce, season to taste with salt and pepper and stir well.

3 Arrange the lettuce leaves and fresh herbs on a serving plate. Run the rice vermicelli under hot water to separate the strands, then drain. Put the vermicelli in the centre of the leaves and cover with the crab mixture. Arrange the quail eggs around the mound and sprinkle with spring onions.

Serves 4

175 g (6 oz) rice vermicelli
2 tablespoons groundnut oil
2 shallots, finely chopped
2 large garlic cloves, finely chopped
375 g (12 oz) crab meat
3 tablespoons hot water
1 tablespoon Vietnamese fish sauce
salt and pepper

To serve:
lettuce leaves
basil, dill and coriander sprigs
8 hard-boiled quail eggs, shelled
2 spring onions, finely sliced

stir-fried noodles with mushrooms

mi xao voi nam rom

4 tablespoons vegetable oil

4 large garlic cloves, finely chopped

2 shallots, finely chopped

2.5 cm (1 inch) piece of fresh root ginger, finely chopped

2–3 small red chillies, finely sliced

6 dried shiitake mushrooms, soaked and sliced

4 pieces dried black fungus, soaked and sliced

185 g (6½ oz) canned straw mushrooms, drained

500 g (1 lb) egg noodles, cooked and set aside

2 tablespoons chopped coriander leaves

1 Heat the oil in a wok and fry the garlic, shallots, ginger and chillies for 30 seconds. Add the shiitake mushrooms, black fungus and straw mushrooms and stir-fry for 1 more minute. Run hot water over the noodles to separate them, add them to the wok and stir-fry quickly to warm them through. Add the coriander leaves, toss and serve.

Serves 4

noodle cakes

bahn hoi

1 Soak the vermicelli in very hot water until done; this will take about 5 minutes. Drain thoroughly – the vermicelli should be as dry as possible – and put it into a mixing bowl and cover with cornflour, making sure it is well coated.

2 Bring some water to the boil in a steamer and grease the steamer rack with some of the oil. Spread some of the noodles out flat over the steamer rack in a thin layer, to make a 25 cm (10 inch) pancake, cover and steam for about 5 minutes. Remove the cake to a board either with a spatula or by inverting the steamer rack.

3 Re-oil the rack and make the next noodle cake. You should make four in all. As the cakes cool down on the board, they form a sort of pancake that you then cut into triangles or squares. Serve warm.

Serves 4

250 g (8 oz) rice vermicelli
60–100 g (2½–3½ oz) cornflour
1 tablespoon vegetable oil

vegetables & salads

Lots of vegetables and salads are consumed in Vietnam. Salad leaves (see Salad Plate, page 56) arrive with most dishes. You can wrap a morsel of this or that, together with a few sprigs of fresh herbs, into a neat salad leaf parcel, dip it into a sauce and pop it into your mouth. Vegetables are seasonal in Vietnam, as they are elsewhere, but the biggest selection is grown around Da Lat where the climate allows for both tropical and temperate crops to be grown.

braised aubergines with minced beef

ca nuong

1 Prick the aubergines several times with a fork and grill or bake in a preheated oven, 190°C (375°F), Gas Mark 5, for about 30 minutes for large ones and 20 minutes for small ones, until they are soft. You do not want to let the skin burn. Allow them to cool, then peel them and cut in half lengthways.

2 While the aubergines are cooking and cooling, mix the minced steak in a bowl with the galangal, fish sauce, pepper and garlic and leave to stand for 30 minutes.

3 Heat the oil in a pan over a high heat and quickly stir-fry the minced steak and all its marinade. Divide the mince into 4 portions.

4 Arrange the aubergines on 4 individual plates and top with the mince. Garnish with coriander sprigs and serve with light soy sauce and fish sauce to taste.

Serves 4

2 large aubergines, weighing about 400 g (13 oz), or 8 small Asian aubergines

125 g (4 oz) rump steak, finely minced

1 cm (½ inch) piece of galangal, finely chopped

2 teaspoons Vietnamese fish sauce

½ teaspoon pepper

1 large garlic clove, crushed and finely chopped

1 teaspoon groundnut oil

coriander sprigs, to garnish

To serve:

light soy sauce

Vietnamese fish sauce

salad plate

sa lach dia

1 round lettuce

1 Cos lettuce

½ cucumber, cut into strips

3 carrots, cut into strips

bean sprouts

spring onions, shredded

fresh herbs, such as coriander, basil, mint and dill

A plate of raw vegetables, salad leaves and fresh herbs is served with almost every meal in Vietnam. They are either added to what you are eating, noodle soup for example, or used to wrap it up, as with grilled pork perhaps, or small pieces of spring roll. This recipe is fairly basic, but you are free to make it as exciting as you like – you can even add pieces of fruit.

1 To serve, wash and dry all the ingredients and arrange them on a large plate in the centre of the table.

Serves 4

pickled carrot strips

goi ca rot

2 large carrots, peeled and cut into long strips with a mandoline or vegetable peeler

4 tablespoons white rice vinegar

175 ml (6 fl oz) cold water

1 tablespoon golden caster sugar

pinch of salt

1 spring onion, shredded

2 tablespoons chopped mixed herbs, such as coriander, basil and mint

1 Combine the carrots, vinegar, water and sugar in a large bowl with a pinch of salt. Cover and refrigerate for 2–3 hours, stirring occasionally.

2 Remove the carrots from the bowl with a slotted spoon and transfer to a serving bowl. Add the spring onion and herbs, mix well and serve immediately.

Serves 4

stir-fried chinese leaves

rao xao co

1 Heat the oil in a wok, add the garlic and stir for about 30 seconds. Add the Chinese leaves and stir-fry for 3–4 minutes. Make a well in the centre of the leaves and pour in the beaten egg and a little fish sauce. Stir the leaves into the egg mixture, starting with those nearest to the egg. Season to taste with salt and pepper.

Serves 4

2 tablespoons groundnut oil

2 garlic cloves, crushed and finely chopped

1 small head Chinese leaves, finely sliced

1 large egg, beaten

splash of Vietnamese fish sauce

salt and pepper

mixed vegetables with lemon grass

rau xeo chay

This dish makes a light main course if it is served with jasmine rice.

vegetable oil, for frying

125 g (4 oz) solid tofu, cut into 1 cm
(½ inch) cubes

3 lemon grass stalks, finely
chopped

2 large garlic cloves, crushed and
finely chopped

1 leek, white part only, thinly sliced

250 g (8 oz) Chinese leaves,
thinly sliced

3 dried shiitake mushrooms,
soaked and sliced

60 g (2½ oz) oyster mushrooms, torn

125 g (4 oz) mangetout

1 bunch of watercress

6 fresh baby corn

1 long mild red chilli, thinly sliced

100 ml (3½ fl oz) Vegetable Stock
(see page 135)

1 tablespoon light soy sauce

1 teaspoon golden granulated sugar

1 tablespoon Vietnamese fish sauce

salt and pepper

1 Heat about 1 cm (½ inch) of oil in a wok and add the tofu cubes. Cook until golden on all sides, then remove and drain on kitchen paper.

2 Drain all but 1 tablespoon of the oil from the wok and reheat it. Add the lemon grass, garlic and leek and stir-fry for about 1 minute, then add the remaining vegetables, a few at a time, stirring constantly. Add the stock, soy sauce, sugar and fish sauce, stir and cover. Cook over a moderate heat for about 6 minutes, stirring occasionally. Stir in the fried tofu, season to taste with salt and pepper and serve hot.

Serves 4

spinach & watercress stir-fry

rau muong xao cac loai

500 g (1 lb) spinach, shredded

2 bunches of watercress, torn

1 tablespoon groundnut oil

3 large garlic cloves, finely minced

2 tablespoons Vietnamese fish sauce

1 Boil some water in a large saucepan and throw in the spinach and watercress. Stir to ensure that all the leaves are cooking equally. They will wilt, shrink and turn a vivid green in about 2–3 minutes. Drain and rinse under cold water to prevent further cooking, then squeeze as much excess water out of the leaves as you can.

2 Heat the oil in a wok, add the garlic and stir-fry until it is just beginning to turn golden. Throw in the spinach and watercress leaves and stir-fry with the garlic until all the leaves are coated with oil and garlic and warmed through. This will take about 2–3 minutes. Splash in the fish sauce, mix thoroughly and serve.

Serves 4

chinese leaf salad

sa lat rau xanh cac loai

1 Put the Chinese leaves, carrot and cucumber into a large salad bowl with the coriander and basil leaves and add mint and chives to taste.

2 Combine all the remaining ingredients in another bowl, mix well and pour over the salad. Toss and serve.

Serves 4

½ **head Chinese leaves, shredded**

½ **carrot, grated, soaked in cold water and dried**

½ **cucumber, deseeded and cubed**

handful of coriander leaves

handful of basil leaves

handful of mint and chives

I spring onion, thinly sliced

2 small red chillies, finely chopped

1 tablespoon Vietnamese fish sauce

juice of 1½ limes

1½ tablespoons golden caster sugar

2 teaspoons white rice vinegar

2 tablespoons cold water

duck & green papaya salad

vit du du

Green papaya seems to be quite hard to find in Britain, but there is no problem finding the really hard papayas with orange flesh that never really ripen. This is a perfect use for those papayas – they do not taste of much in themselves, but neither do the green, unripe ones. The papaya shreds take on the tastes of the other ingredients.

2 duck breast fillets, skin and fat removed

1 garlic clove, finely chopped

1 dessertspoon golden caster sugar

75 ml (3 fl oz) white rice vinegar

1 small red chilli, finely chopped

pinch of salt

2 small, hard papayas, peeled and shredded, or 1 green papaya

Marinade:

2 teaspoons clear honey

1 shallot, finely chopped

2 garlic cloves, finely chopped

1 lemon grass stalk, finely chopped

pinch of five spice powder

pinch of ground cinnamon

1 small red chilli, finely chopped

salt and pepper

To garnish:

chopped coriander leaves

Crushed Roasted Peanuts (see page 141)

1 To make the marinade, mix together all the ingredients in a bowl. Add the duck fillets, cover and leave to marinate for 2–3 hours.

2 Arrange the duck fillets with their marinade in a roasting tin and roast in a preheated oven, 150°C (300°F), Gas Mark 2, for 1 hour. Remove the duck fillets and allow to cool, then cut into slices.

3 In a large bowl, mix together the garlic, sugar, vinegar, chilli and salt. Add the papaya shreds and mix them in well, then add the duck slices. To serve, sprinkle with coriander leaves and peanuts.

Serves 4

poultry & game

Chickens and ducks in Vietnam are usually tougher, hardier and tastier birds than those we are used to. They range around all day long, eating whatever they can find. Poultry, like other types of meat, is quite expensive for the average Vietnamese purse, and the quantities eaten are small in comparison to what we have come to expect in the West. In the upland regions of central and northern Vietnam there is still plenty of game to be found and, if you are lucky, you will be able to sit down to a meal of pheasant, quail or partridge.

chicken & lemon grass curry

cari ga xoa lan

1 Heat the oil in a wok, add the garlic and shallots and stir-fry for 1 minute. Add the lemon grass, fish sauce, pepper, sugar, curry paste, chillies and chicken strips and stir-fry for 3–4 minutes.

2 Add the stock and coconut milk, mix well and simmer gently for 6 minutes, or until the chicken is cooked through. Serve garnished with peanuts and coriander leaves.

Serves 4

2 tablespoons groundnut oil

2 garlic cloves, finely chopped

3 shallots, finely sliced

3 lemon grass stalks, crushed and cut into 2.5 cm (1 inch) pieces

2 tablespoons Vietnamese fish sauce

½ teaspoon pepper

½ teaspoon palm or golden granulated sugar

1 teaspoon mild curry paste, such as korma or Thai yellow curry paste

2 small green chillies, chopped

750 g (1½ lb) boneless, skinless chicken breasts, cut into 5 mm x 2.5 cm (¼ x 1 inch) strips

3 tablespoons Chicken Stock (see page 134)

125 ml (4 fl oz) coconut milk

To garnish:

2 tablespoons Crushed Roasted Peanuts (see page 141)

handful of coriander leaves

chicken curry

cari ga

1 First make the marinade. Grind all the ingredients briefly in a small food processor, then pound them in a mortar. This releases more of their juices. Spread this marinade over the chicken pieces, cover and leave for a minimum of 3 hours at room temperature or preferably overnight in the refrigerator.

2 Heat half the oil in a heavy-based casserole, add the potato pieces and brown them all over. Remove and drain on kitchen paper. Add the remaining oil to the casserole and add the chicken pieces, browning the skin.

3 Add the crushed lemon grass stalks and return the potatoes with half the water. Open both cans of coconut milk, spoon out and reserve the thickest part, and add the rest to the casserole. Mix well, bring almost to the boil, then lower the heat and simmer for 40 minutes, stirring occasionally. Add the remaining water if you think it is becoming too thick.

4 Mix the sugar with the thick coconut cream and add to the casserole just before serving. Season to taste with salt. Garnish the curry with coriander leaves, spring onions and lime wedges and serve with French bread.

Serves 4

1.5 kg (3 lb) chicken, cut into 8 pieces

125 ml (4 fl oz) groundnut oil

1 kg (2 lb) potatoes, chopped into pieces

2 lemon grass stalks, crushed

250 ml (8 fl oz) water (optional)

2 x 400 ml (14 fl oz) cans coconut milk

1 teaspoon palm or golden granulated sugar

salt and pepper

French bread, to serve

Marinade:

1 onion, roughly chopped

4 garlic cloves, crushed and chopped

2.5 cm (1 inch) piece of galangal, finely chopped

3 lemon grass stalks, finely sliced

1 teaspoon dried chilli

2 teaspoons mild curry paste

To garnish:

handful of coriander leaves

4 spring onions, diagonally sliced

lime wedges

saigon roast chicken

ga saigon

1 Mix all the marinade ingredients together thoroughly, then rub the marinade all over the chicken. Put the onion and lemon half inside the chicken, along with any remaining marinade. Cover and leave to marinate overnight in the refrigerator.

2 Place the chicken, breast side up, on a rack in a roasting tin and roast in a preheated oven, 160°C (325°F), Gas Mark 3, for 40 minutes, then turn the chicken over and roast for a further 40 minutes.

3 Finally, increase the heat to 220°C (425°F), Gas Mark 7, turn the chicken so that it is breast side up again and roast for 20 minutes, until it is cooked through. Remove the chicken from the oven and allow it to stand for 10 minutes before carving. Serve with the sauce for dipping.

Serves 4

1.5 kg (3 lb) chicken
1 small onion
½ lemon
Lime and Ginger Sauce (see page 140), to serve

Marinade:
2 shallots, finely chopped
6 garlic cloves, finely chopped
60 g (2½ oz) lemon grass, finely chopped
juice of ½ lemon
2 tablespoons Vietnamese fish sauce
3 tablespoons light soy sauce
1 teaspoon pepper
4 tablespoons clear honey
125 ml (4 fl oz) vegetable oil

grilled lime chicken

ga chanh roti

1 Mix the chicken in a bowl with the honey, fish sauce and salt and pepper. Leave to stand.

2 In a small food processor, mix the spring onions, garlic and lime leaves, adding a little water if necessary. Make sure the lime paste is completely smooth, then add to the chicken. Stir well then cover and marinate for 2 hours.

3 Cover a grill rack with foil, add the chicken pieces and brush with oil. Place under a preheated grill and cook, turning from time to time, for about 15 minutes, or until the chicken is cooked through. Keep brushing with the oil and any remaining marinade.

4 Garnish the chicken with mint leaves and serve with rice, lime wedges and the dipping sauce.

Serves 4

375 g (12 oz) boneless, skinless chicken breast, cut into 2.5 cm (1 inch) cubes

2 teaspoons clear honey

2 teaspoons Vietnamese fish sauce

2 spring onions, chopped

2 garlic cloves, chopped

16 kaffir lime leaves, shredded

vegetable oil, for brushing

salt and pepper

handful of mint leaves, to garnish

To serve:

rice

lime wedges

Nuoc Cham Dipping Sauce (see page 141)

chicken with orange & honey

ga nuong cam

1 shallot, finely sliced

6 large garlic cloves, finely sliced

2.5 cm (1 inch) piece of fresh root ginger, finely chopped

2 tablespoons clear honey

1 teaspoon pepper

1 tablespoon dark soy sauce

2½ tablespoons Vietnamese fish sauce

2 teaspoons sesame oil

1 tablespoon Chinese rice wine

1 teaspoon grated orange rind

juice of 1 large orange

1 tablespoon groundnut oil

8 chicken thighs

1 Put the shallot, garlic and ginger into a mortar and pound to a paste. Add all the remaining ingredients except for the chicken thighs and blend together thoroughly. This can be done in a small blender.

2 Place the chicken in a bowl and cover with the marinade, making sure each piece is well coated. Cover and leave in the refrigerator overnight.

3 Transfer the chicken pieces with all the marinade to a roasting tin and roast, skin side up, in a preheated oven, 160°C (325°F), Gas Mark 3, for 30 minutes. Increase the heat to 220°C (425°F), Gas Mark 7 and cook for a further 20 minutes, until the skin is crispy and the chicken is cooked through.

Serves 4

grilled chicken with lemon grass

ga xoa lan

1 First butterfly the chicken breasts. Slit each one horizontally, so that it is still joined at one side then open it out. Cover it with clingfilm and bash it flat with a meat mallet or a rolling pin.

2 Combine the lemon grass, garlic, sugar, soy and fish sauces, lemon juice and groundnut oil in a bowl, mix thoroughly, then coat the chicken. Cover and leave to marinate for at least 1 hour.

3 Place the chicken breasts on a grill rack and cook under a preheated grill for about 3 minutes on each side, or until cooked through. Slice and serve.

Serves 4

2 large boneless, skinless chicken breasts

1½ lemon grass stalks, very finely chopped

2 large garlic cloves, finely chopped

2 teaspoons palm or golden granulated sugar

2 teaspoons light soy sauce

1 teaspoon Vietnamese fish sauce

juice of ½ lemon

2 tablespoons groundnut oil

caramel ginger chicken

ga caramen voi xot gung

1 Heat the oil in a wok until very hot, add the shallot, garlic, chillies and ginger and stir-fry for 1 minute. Add the chicken strips, reduce the heat and stir-fry for 4 minutes.

2 Add the caramel syrup, chicken stock and fish sauce, mix well, turn the heat to low and cook for 10–15 minutes, or until the chicken is cooked through. Just before serving, add the spring onions and stir once. Garnish with coriander leaves and serve with rice.

Serves 4

2 tablespoons groundnut oil

½ large shallot, chopped

2 large garlic cloves, finely chopped

3 small green chillies, finely chopped

100 g (3½ oz) fresh root ginger, finely chopped

750 g (1½ lb) boneless, skinless chicken, cut into 5 mm x 2.5 cm (¼ x 1 inch) strips

125–150 ml (4–5 fl oz) Caramel Syrup (see page 142)

4 tablespoons Chicken Stock (see page 134)

2 tablespoons Vietnamese fish sauce

2 spring onions, sliced lengthways, then cut into 2.5 cm (1 inch) strips

handful of coriander leaves, to garnish

boiled rice, to serve

steamed chicken with shiitake mushrooms

nam dong cotiem ga

1 Cut the mushrooms into thin strips and put them into a heatproof bowl with the chicken. Add all the remaining ingredients and mix thoroughly.

2 Cover the bowl with foil and place it in a steamer over boiling water. Steam for 40 minutes, making sure to top up the water in the steamer now and again. Serve on a warmed platter, garnished with the coriander leaves.

Serves 4

6 shiitake mushrooms (soaked if dried)

750 g (1½ lb) boneless, skinless chicken breast, cut into small, thin strips

1 tablespoon finely chopped fresh root ginger

3 spring onions, diagonally sliced

1 teaspoon pepper

1 tablespoon Vietnamese fish sauce

2 garlic cloves, finely chopped

1 teaspoon sesame oil

pinch of salt

coriander leaves, to garnish

quail & oyster mushrooms

chim cut uop voi nam rom

If you do not want to spatchcock the quails yourself, ask your butcher to do it for you. They are usually happy to do this if you ask them in advance. Coconut water is the liquid which you find sloshing around inside a coconut. You can buy it in cans in oriental shops.

1 First spatchcock the quails. Place each bird, breast side down, on a chopping board and cut through the backbone. Open out the bird and flatten it with a meat mallet. Thread two long metal skewers across the body of each bird to hold it flat.

2 Put the shallots, garlic, white pepper, cinnamon, five spice powder, fish sauce and oyster sauce into a mortar and pound until well amalgamated. Marinate the quails in the mixture overnight. Remove the skewers.

3 Heat the oil in a large frying pan, add the quails with all their marinade and stir-fry for about 5 minutes. Add the oyster mushrooms and stir-fry for another 2 minutes. Add the coconut water and simmer, covered, on a low heat for 15 minutes.

Serves 4

4 oven-ready quails

3 shallots, chopped

2 garlic cloves, chopped

pinch of white pepper

pinch of cinnamon

½ teaspoon five spice powder

1 teaspoon Vietnamese fish sauce

1 tablespoon oyster sauce

2 tablespoons groundnut oil

250 g (8 oz) oyster mushrooms, torn

125 ml (4 fl oz) coconut water

vietnamese roast duck

vit quay

In order to achieve nice crisp skin, the duck needs to be dry. You could spend a few minutes, while you are heating the oven, blow-drying it with a hairdryer.

1 Place the duck in a shallow roasting tin and prick it several times with a fork, to allow the fat to escape. Pound all the remaining ingredients together in a mortar and rub this marinade into the duck, making sure every inch is covered. Pour some into the cavity as well, then refrigerate, uncovered, for at least 8 hours.

2 Roast the duck in a preheated oven, 220°C (425°F), Gas Mark 7, for about 1½ hours, until dark brown and crispy. Pour off the fat from the tin during the roasting time.

3 Allow the duck to cool down a bit, then cut it in half, through the backbone, using a cleaver or poultry shears. Chop the breast into 5–6 slices, and joint the legs. Serve each piece of duck with some crispy skin and rice. Garnish with spring onion slices.

Serves 4

1.5 kg (3 lb) duck

6 garlic cloves, crushed and chopped

1 teaspoon pepper

½ teaspoon salt

½ teaspoon five spice powder

3 tablespoons dark soy sauce

1 tablespoon sesame oil

1 tablespoon Chinese rice wine

boiled rice, to serve

spring onion slices, to garnish

duck congee

chao vit

1 duck leg

1 litre (1¾ pints) water

1 teaspoon vegetable oil

1 large garlic clove, finely chopped

1 small red chilli, finely sliced
(optional)

125 g (4 oz) Thai jasmine rice

salt and pepper

chopped coriander leaves,
to garnish

This dish is often eaten for breakfast. Unlike the Thais or Chinese, the Vietnamese usually make their congee with whole grains rather than broken grains of rice.

1 Put the duck into a heavy-based saucepan with the water, bring to the boil and simmer for about 20 minutes. Remove the duck to a plate, reserving the stock in the saucepan. When the duck is cool enough, remove the skin and fat, and tear the meat into shreds.

2 Oil a wok and, when it is warm, add the garlic and chilli, if using, and stir-fry briefly. Add the rice and stir gently over a low heat for about 10 minutes, or until the rice is turning golden.

3 Add the rice mixture to the duck stock with a pinch of salt and pepper. Cover the saucepan and cook gently until the rice is soft, but not dry – about 15–20 minutes. Do not stir too often, as you do not want to break the grains of rice. When it is ready, stir in the duck and serve, garnished with the coriander leaves.

Serves 4

twice-cooked duck with ginger sauce

thit vit voi xot gung

1 Prick the duck all over with a fork and place on a rack over a roasting tin. Roast the duck in a preheated oven, 180°C (350°C), Gas Mark 4, for about 1½ hours, until tender.

2 Meanwhile, make the marinade. Combine the garlic, ginger, five spice powder, chilli sauce and groundnut oil in a bowl.

3 Allow the duck to cool and then cut it in half down the backbone, using a cleaver or poultry shears. Remove the ribs and backbone. Place the duck on a dish and cover it with the marinade. Cover and refrigerate overnight.

4 Put the duck, skin side up, on a wire rack over a roasting tin. Roast, uncovered, in a preheated oven, 200°C (400°F), Gas Mark 6, for about 35 minutes, until the skin is crisp.

5 While the duck is roasting, simmer all the ingredients for the ginger sauce in a saucepan until reduced to about half. Strain and return to the pan. Serve the duck sprinkled with spring onions and with the sauce poured around it.

Serves 4

1.5 kg (3 lb) duck
thinly sliced spring onions, to garnish

Marinade:

2 garlic cloves, crushed and chopped

1 tablespoon finely chopped ginger

½ teaspoon five spice powder

2 tablespoons Quick Sweet Chilli Sauce (see page 142)

1 tablespoon groundnut oil

Ginger sauce:

750 ml (1¼ pints) Vegetable Stock (see page 135)

1 orange, cut into pieces

2 pieces dried orange peel (optional)

125 g (4 oz) fresh root ginger, sliced

2 tablespoons palm or golden granulated sugar

duck with pineapple

vit ham thom

1 To make the marinade, mix together the garlic, shallots and fish sauce in a bowl and add the duck fillets. Rub the duck with the mixture, cover and leave for 3 hours.

2 Heat a little groundnut oil in a wok and fry the duck and its marinade until the shallots have softened. Add the onions, shiitake mushrooms and green chillies and stir-fry for 2 minutes, then add the stock, pineapple and mild red chilli. Bring to the boil, season to taste with salt and pepper, then reduce the heat and simmer, covered, for 40 minutes.

3 Serve the duck on warmed plates garnished with coriander sprigs and crushed roasted peanuts.

Serves 4

2 duck breast fillets, skinned

groundnut oil, for frying

2 onions, chopped

8 dried shiitake mushrooms, soaked and thinly sliced

2 small green chillies, finely sliced

600 ml (1 pint) Chicken Stock (see page 134)

250 g (8 oz) fresh pineapple, cut into chunks

1 long mild red chilli, diagonally sliced

salt and pepper

Marinade:

3 large garlic cloves, finely chopped

4 shallots, finely chopped

2 tablespoons Vietnamese fish sauce

To garnish:

coriander sprigs

Crushed Roasted Peanuts (see page 141)

duck with yogurt sauce

vit nuong toi

4 duck legs

4 tablespoons water

150 g (5 oz) natural yogurt

salt and pepper

watercress sprigs, to garnish

Marinade:

1 tablespoon Vietnamese fish sauce

100 ml (3½ fl oz) red rice vinegar

3 large garlic cloves, crushed
and chopped

1 onion, finely chopped

12 juniper berries, crushed

2 teaspoons fennel seeds

This is a recipe that clearly shows the French influence on Vietnamese cuisine.

1 To make the marinade, mix together the fish sauce, vinegar, garlic, onion, juniper berries and fennel seeds in a bowl. Put the duck legs into the marinade, cover and leave overnight in the refrigerator.

2 Put the duck legs, skin side down, in a roasting tin, reserving as much of the marinade as you can. Cook in a preheated oven, 220°C (425°F), Gas Mark 7, for 30 minutes, basting occasionally, then turn the duck over and roast for another 30 minutes, basting at least once with the juices in the pan. Turn off the oven, but leave the duck in it while you make the sauce.

3 Spoon the marinade into a saucepan, add the water and simmer until the onion is soft. Strain the sauce through a sieve into another pan, pushing through as much onion as you can. Add the yogurt, season to taste with salt and pepper and stir. Divide the sauce between 4 warmed plates and serve the duck on it, with a little watercress on the side.

Serves 4

five spice pheasant

ga xoi mo

1 Combine the salt and five spice powder in a bowl and rub the pheasants all over with the mixture. Cover and marinate for at least 3 hours at room temperature or overnight in the refrigerator.

2 Put the tamarind water, fish sauce and sugar into a small saucepan and bring to the boil. Remove from the heat, add the garlic and chillies, stir and set aside.

3 Pour enough oil into a deep-fryer to cover the pheasants. Heat the oil to 190°C (375°F), then carefully add the birds and reduce the heat to 160°C (325°F). You may only be able to get one or two pieces of pheasant in at a time. Fry the pheasant pieces for 5 minutes on each side, or until their juices run clear. When they are cooked through and crispy, transfer to kitchen paper. Keep them warm in a low oven if you have to cook them in batches.

4 Either pull the meat off the bones with a fork or cut the birds into smaller serving pieces. Serve with the tamarind sauce in individual dipping bowls, rice and a salad plate.

Serves 4

1 teaspoon salt

1 teaspoon five spice powder

2 hen pheasants, halved

2 teaspoons tamarind concentrate, dissolved in 300 ml (½ pint) hot water

4 tablespoons Vietnamese fish sauce

100 g (3½ oz) palm or golden granulated sugar

5 large garlic cloves, finely chopped

2 small red chillies, finely chopped

oil, for deep-frying

To serve:

boiled rice

Salad Plate, including mint and dill (see page 56)

steamboat duck

lau vit

1 Place the duck fillets, side by side, in a shallow pan and just cover with some of the stock. Cook, covered, for 30 minutes, or until tender. Remove and cut into thick slices.

2 Meanwhile, cook the sweet potato in boiling water for about 10 minutes, until tender. Drain and reserve. Cook the rice noodles, drain and reserve.

3 Bring the remaining stock to the boil and pour it into a steamboat or fondue pot. Place it over a flame on the table. Divide the duck and sweet potato chunks between 4 bowls. Bring all the other ingredients to the table in separate bowls and arrange around the steamboat. Each person helps themselves, warming their noodles and cooking their vegetables in the simmering stock, and adding chillies, peanuts and coriander to taste. At the end of the meal, the broth can be drunk.

Serves 4

2 skinless duck breast fillets

1.8 litres (3 pints) Chicken Stock (see page 134)

500 g (1 lb) sweet potatoes, cut into chunks

250 g (8 oz) rice noodles

4 spring onions, finely sliced

500 g (1 lb) spinach

250 g (8 oz) bok choi

4 small red chillies, finely sliced

4 tablespoons Crushed Roasted Peanuts (see page 141)

handful of coriander sprigs

meat

There are plenty of pigs in Vietnam, and lots of pork is eaten. A great many Vietnamese dishes require finely minced meat – the vast majority of which is pork. They also eat pork in the form of chops and spare ribs, and as slow-cooked stews and a delicious pâté which is quite unlike a Western one. Pork has an affinity with sweetness, and the Vietnamese use of caramelized sauces proves the point. Beef is something of a treat in Vietnam. In reality, quite a lot of the meat that is served as beef is actually buffalo and sometimes venison. Beef is so highly thought of that there is a special traditional banquet, called 'Seven Styles of Beef', for which seven completely different beef dishes are prepared. Unlike any other banquet or formal dinner, these dishes are presented sequentially, each one enhancing the next.

paddyfield pork

thit kho

100 g (3½ oz) light muscovado sugar

125 ml (4 fl oz) Vietnamese
fish sauce

4 tablespoons chopped shallots

2 garlic cloves, chopped

1 teaspoon pepper

500 g (1 lb) boneless pork loin,
thinly sliced

4 hard-boiled eggs, shelled
and halved

Chinese chive flowers, to garnish

rice, to serve

1 Heat the sugar in a small casserole over a low heat until it is melted, stirring constantly. Slowly add the fish sauce and keep stirring vigorously until it is all amalgamated.

2 Add the shallots, garlic, pepper and pork slices to the caramel, cover and simmer over a low heat for about 30 minutes, giving it an occasional stir around.

3 To serve, arrange the sliced pork on a warmed platter with the eggs and pour over the sauce, covering the eggs as well as the pork. Garnish with Chinese chive flowers and serve a dish of rice on the side.

Serves 4

easy one-dish pork

bun xoa thit

1 Heat the oil in a wok, add the shallots and garlic and stir-fry until they are soft.

2 Add the chilli, pork strips and fish sauce and season with salt and pepper. Stir-fry for 10–15 minutes, until the pork is turning golden.

3 Bring the coconut milk gently to the boil in a small saucepan and, while it is heating, divide the vermicelli between 4 large bowls. Divide the pork mixture between the bowls and pour the coconut milk over the top. Serve with the peanuts, coriander leaves and the dipping sauce.

Serves 4

1 tablespoon groundnut oil

8 shallots, finely chopped

4 large garlic cloves, finely chopped

1 small red chilli, finely sliced

250 g (8 oz) boneless pork, cut into small strips

splash of Vietnamese fish sauce

300 ml (½ pint) coconut milk

250 g (8 oz) rice vermicelli, cooked and drained

salt and pepper

To serve:

Crushed Roasted Peanuts (see page 141)

coriander leaves

Nuoc Cham Dipping Sauce (see page 141)

spicy pork chops

thit heo nuong vi

1 First make the marinade. Put the garlic, sugar, peppercorns, lemon grass, fish sauce, rice wine, sesame oil and groundnut oil into a small food processor and work to a paste. If you prefer you can pound the first 4 ingredients to a paste in a mortar and add the next 4 ingredients to the paste, little by little, as you pound. Mix it all thoroughly.

2 Place the pork chops in a shallow dish and cover them completely with the marinade. Cover the dish and leave to marinate in the refrigerator overnight.

3 Transfer the chops to a grill rack and cook under a preheated grill for about 8 minutes on each side, until brown. Try not to put the chops too close to the heat or the outsides will burn before the insides are done. Serve the chops garnished with coriander and with the dipping sauce.

Serves 4

4 x 250 g (8 oz) loin pork chops

coriander sprigs, to garnish

Nuoc Cham Dipping Sauce (see page 141), to serve

Marinade:

3 garlic cloves

2 tablespoons palm or light muscovado sugar

15 black peppercorns

1 lemon grass stalk, roughly chopped

2 tablespoons Vietnamese fish sauce

1 tablespoon Chinese rice wine

1 teaspoon sesame oil

2 tablespoons groundnut oil

cinnamon pâté

cha que

This is a pâté which is eaten a lot in Vietnam. Although it shows the strong French influence that there has been on the national cuisine, it is very different from the sort of pâtés we are accustomed to in Europe. European pâtés are made using quite a lot of fat, and we can often spread them on toast or a biscuit. This one is fat free, dense and firm, more like a meat loaf.

1 Oil a loaf tin. Put all the ingredients into a food processor and process until they are very finely ground. You can add 2–3 tablespoons of cold water if the mixture is difficult to process.

2 Pour the mixture into the loaf tin and bake in a preheated oven, 180°C (350°F), Gas Mark 4, for about 45 minutes until cooked through and firm to the touch.

3 Allow the pâté to cool in the tin, then turn it out on to a plate. Sprinkle the top with the chopped herbs. Serve the pâté in thin slices, with salad leaves and French bread.

Serves 4

500 g (1 lb) very lean leg of pork, cut into 2.5 cm (1 inch) cubes

½ teaspoon ground cinnamon

3 tablespoons Vietnamese fish sauce

1 teaspoon palm or golden granulated sugar

1 teaspoon cornflour

1½ teaspoons baking powder

1 teaspoon pepper

1½ teaspoons groundnut oil

handful of basil and coriander leaves, finely chopped, to garnish

To serve:

salad leaves

French bread

hanoi grilled pork

bun cha

1 Gently melt the light muscovado sugar with two-thirds of the fish sauce in a heavy-based saucepan, stirring all the time. Allow to cool a little then transfer it to a bowl and combine it with the garlic, shallot, palm or caster sugar, the remaining fish sauce and salt. Add the minced pork, mix thoroughly, then cover and leave to stand for 3 hours.

2 Shape the minced pork into 20–24 flat little patties, about 2.5 cm (1 inch) in diameter, place them under a preheated grill and cook for 3–4 minutes on each side, until cooked through. The patties are also very good cooked on a barbecue.

3 To serve, divide the noodles between 4 warmed bowls, add the pork, torn lettuce leaves, bean sprouts and herbs. Spoon the dipping sauce over the whole lot.

Serves 4

1 tablespoon light muscovado
sugar

2 tablespoons Vietnamese
fish sauce

1 large garlic clove, finely chopped

1 large shallot, finely chopped

2 teaspoons palm or golden
caster sugar

1 teaspoon salt

500 g (1 lb) boneless pork
loin, minced

250 g (8 oz) rice noodles, cooked

lettuce leaves, torn

125 g (4 oz) bean sprouts

handful of coriander, basil leaves,
mint leaves and chives

Cucumber Dipping Sauce (see page
143), to serve

vietnamese sweet pork

thit lon nau caramen kieu vietnam

1 Gently heat the sugar with the water in a heavy-based casserole until the sugar is dissolved and the mixture is beginning to thicken and caramelize a little.

2 Add the pork, sliced radish, pepper and shallot and top up the casserole with water, level with the ingredients. Add the fish sauce, stir and bring to the boil. Reduce the heat to a simmer, cover and continue to simmer for 1–1½ hours, or until the pork is tender and cooked through.

Serves 4

50 g (2 oz) palm or golden granulated sugar

2 tablespoons water

500 g (1 lb) lean leg of pork, cubed

1 mooli radish, about 30 cm (12 inches) long, peeled and thinly sliced

1 teaspoon pepper

1 shallot, chopped

100 ml (3½ fl oz) Vietnamese fish sauce

grilled pork skewers

nem nuong

These pork skewers are very good cooked on the barbecue.

1 Put all the ingredients into a bowl and mix thoroughly. Cover and leave to marinate overnight in the refrigerator.

2 Soak 16 bamboo skewers in water for about 20 minutes, then form the pork mixture around them.

3 Cook the pork skewers under a preheated grill for about 10 minutes, turning them frequently. To eat, remove the meat from the skewers, wrap it up in salad leaves and dip into the sauce.

Serves 4

500 g (1 lb) finely minced pork

1 teaspoon pepper

3 large garlic cloves, finely minced

1½ tablespoons golden caster sugar

2½ teaspoons cornflour

2 tablespoons Vietnamese fish sauce

To serve:

Salad Plate (see page 56)

Nuoc Cham Dipping Sauce (see page 141)

vietnamese lemon grass spareribs

xuong nuong xa vietnam

Ask your butcher to give you good, meaty spareribs, cut in half. These spareribs take some time to cook, but the end result is worth the effort.

1 Arrange the spareribs in one layer in a large roasting tin, cover with water and bring slowly to the boil. Add the star anise and crushed lemon grass, cover with foil and simmer in a preheated oven, 150–160°C (300–325°F), Gas Mark 2–3, for 2 hours.

2 While the ribs are simmering, make a marinade. In a large mortar, pound together the garlic, shallots, pepper, salt, sugar, fish sauce, rice wine, lemon grass and oil, or process them in a food processor.

3 Remove the spareribs from the oven, drain and pat dry with kitchen paper. Turn up the oven heat to 220°C (425°F), Gas Mark 7. Put the ribs back into the clean, dry, roasting tin while they are still hot and coat them well with the marinade. Roast them on the top shelf of the oven for 30 minutes, until they are brown and crusty looking.

Serves 4

1 kg (2 lb) spareribs

3 star anise

3 lemon grass stalks, crushed

8 garlic cloves

2 large shallots, finely chopped

1 heaped teaspoon pepper

1 teaspoon salt

3 tablespoons palm sugar

2 tablespoons Vietnamese fish sauce

1 tablespoon Chinese rice wine

4 lemon grass stalks, finely chopped

1 tablespoon groundnut oil

vietnamese grilled pork

thit nuong

1 To make the marinade, combine the garlic, shallots, sugar, pepper, fish sauce, rice wine and groundnut oil.

2 Place the pork slices in a bowl and coat thoroughly with the marinade. Cover and leave in the refrigerator overnight.

3 Thread the pork slices on to 8 pre-soaked bamboo skewers in a zig-zag fashion and cook under a preheated grill for about 4 minutes on each side, or until cooked through.

4 Serve the skewers with noodles, peanuts, salad and nuoc cham dipping sauce.

Serves 4

500 g (1 lb) lean pork loin, cut into thin slices

Marinade:

3 large garlic cloves, chopped

3 large shallots, chopped

1 tablespoon palm or light muscovado sugar

1 teaspoon pepper

2 tablespoons Vietnamese fish sauce

1 tablespoon Chinese rice wine

2 tablespoons groundnut oil

To serve:

rice noodles

Crushed Roasted Peanuts (see page 141)

Salad Plate (see page 56)

Nuoc Cham Dipping Sauce (see page 141)

grilled lemon grass beef

bo nuong sa ot

1 Put the lemon grass, shallots, chillies, garlic, salt, pepper and oil in a mortar and pound together, or process in a small food processor. Mix well with the beef, cover and marinate at room temperature for at least 3 hours.

2 Thread the beef cubes on to pre-soaked bamboo skewers. Cook under a preheated hot grill for about 3 minutes on each side, turning occasionally. Serve with the salad, dipping sauce and pieces of French bread.

Serves 4

4 lemon grass stalks, finely chopped

4 large shallots, finely chopped

2 small red chillies, finely chopped

3 large garlic cloves, finely chopped

1 teaspoon salt

1 teaspoon pepper

1 tablespoon groundnut oil

750 g (1½ lb) lean rump steak, cut into 1 cm (½ inch) cubes

To serve:

Salad Plate (see page 56)

Nuoc Cham Dipping Sauce (see page 141)

French bread

shaky beef

bo luc lac

1 Mix the garlic, soy sauce, sugar, rice wine, spring onion and pepper with half the oil in a large bowl and add the steak. Mix well, cover and leave in the refrigerator overnight.

2 Heat the remaining oil in a large frying pan and, when it is just beginning to smoke, put in the beef cubes, in one layer. Cook, without stirring, for about 1 minute – there should be a thin crust at the bottom. Shake the pan vigorously to loosen the beef (use tongs or chopsticks if you need to) and continue to cook, shaking the pan every so often, until the beef is cooked to your taste. Allow 4 minutes for medium-done beef. Serve with the sauce, rice and salad.

Serves 4

6 large garlic cloves, finely chopped

2 tablespoons dark soy sauce

2 tablespoons palm or light muscovado sugar

2 tablespoons Chinese rice wine

1 spring onion, finely chopped

1 teaspoon pepper

4 tablespoons groundnut oil

750 g (1½ lb) rump steak, cut into 2.5 cm (1 inch) cubes

To serve:

Lime and Ginger Sauce (see page 140)

rice

Chinese Leaf Salad (see page 61)

fillet of beef with sesame seeds

bit tet xao me

1 Mix the garlic, soy sauce, fish sauce, sesame oil, sugar, pepper and chillies in a bowl with 1 tablespoon of the groundnut oil. Add the beef slices, mix thoroughly and leave to marinate, covered, in the refrigerator overnight.

2 Heat the remaining oil in a wok or frying pan and, when it is very hot, add the beef slices in one layer. Cook quickly, about 1½ minutes on each side for medium-done beef, and remove to a warmed plate. Cover and keep warm while you cook the remaining slices, if you could not fit them all in at once. Sprinkle with the sesame seeds, garnish with chives and serve with rice and the spinach and watercress stir-fry.

Serves 4

4 large garlic cloves, finely minced

1½ tablespoons light soy sauce

1 tablespoon Vietnamese fish sauce

1 teaspoon sesame oil

1 tablespoon palm or golden granulated sugar

1 teaspoon pepper

3 small red chillies, finely chopped

2 tablespoons groundnut oil

500 g (1 lb) fillet of beef, thinly sliced

2 teaspoons sesame seeds, toasted

Chinese chives, to garnish

To serve:

rice

Spinach & Watercress Stir-fry (see page 60)

beef with bamboo shoots

bo xao mang

1 Heat half of the oil in a wok and fry the garlic and chilli for about 30 seconds. Add the steak and cook for 1 minute, stirring, then remove the meat and set aside.

2 Heat the remaining oil in the wok, add the bamboo shoots and spring onions and stir-fry for 1–2 minutes. Add the fish sauce and water and bring the sauce to the boil. Add the steak and any juices it has made. Stir well to warm the steak through. Transfer it to a warmed serving dish and sprinkle with sesame seeds and basil leaves.

Serves 4

4 tablespoons groundnut oil

2 large garlic cloves, finely chopped

1 small red chilli, finely sliced

500 g (1 lb) lean rump steak, thinly sliced

225 g (7½ oz) bamboo shoots, drained and sliced

4 spring onions, finely sliced

2 tablespoons Vietnamese fish sauce

2 tablespoons water

To garnish:

3 tablespoons sesame seeds, toasted

basil leaves

grilled peanut beef

thit bo xien xot

1 Put the cubes of steak into a large bowl with the shallot, garlic, lemon grass, ginger, mint, fish sauce and oil. Mix together thoroughly, then cover and leave to marinate in the refrigerator overnight.

2 Combine the peanuts, pepper and dried chillies in a flat dish. Thread the cubes of steak on to pre-soaked bamboo skewers and roll them in the peanut mixture.

3 Brush a little oil on to the meat with a pastry brush and cook under a preheated hot grill for 6–8 minutes, turning frequently. Serve with the dipping sauce.

Serves 4

750 g (1½ lb) lean rump steak, cut into 2.5 cm (1 inch) cubes

1 large shallot, finely chopped

3 garlic cloves, crushed and finely chopped

½ lemon grass stalk, finely chopped

1 tablespoon finely chopped ginger

2 heaped tablespoons finely chopped mint leaves

4 tablespoons Vietnamese fish sauce

1 tablespoon groundnut oil

150 g (5 oz) Crushed Roasted Peanuts (see page 141)

1 tablespoon roughly ground black pepper

1 teaspoon crushed dried chillies

vegetable oil, for brushing

Quick Sweet Chilli Sauce (see page 142), to serve

vietnamese steak tartare

bit te ta ta

This dish is an example of the French influence on Vietnamese cuisine. It would have been eaten by wealthy, cosmopolitan members of society. Suitable accompaniments are Chinese Leaf Salad (see page 61) and French fries.

1 To serve, place the steak in a mound in the centre of a large platter. Put all the other ingredients into small bowls or ramekins and arrange them around the steak. The diners can then help themselves to the meat and mix their own steak tartare.

Serves 4

750 g (1½ lb) fillet steak, finely minced

30 basil leaves, finely chopped

30 mint leaves, finely chopped

large handful of coriander leaves, finely chopped

3 large garlic cloves, finely chopped

4 thin slices galangal, finely chopped

2 large shallots, finely chopped

4 small green chillies, finely sliced

Vietnamese fish sauce

4 egg yolks in half shells (optional)

salt and pepper

Lime and Ginger Sauce (see page 140)

vietnamese beef stew

bo kho

As with all stews, this one tastes best if you have time to cook it on one day, allow it to cool and refrigerate it overnight, then reheat it the next day.

1 In a bowl, combine the beef with the five spice powder, pepper, half the lemon grass, 2 of the garlic cloves, the salt, soy sauce and sugar. Mix well, cover and leave to marinate for at least 1 hour.

2 Heat the oil in a casserole or heavy-based saucepan and, when it is hot, brown the beef cubes. Add the shallot, the remaining garlic and the lemon grass and stir-fry for about 1 minute, then add the tomatoes. Finally, add the carrots, star anise, cinnamon stick, chillies and water. Bring slowly to the boil, turn down the heat and simmer for about 2 hours, or until the beef is very tender. This can be done either in a preheated oven, 180–190°C (350–375°F), Gas Mark 4–5, or on the hob. Garnish with basil leaves and serve with French bread.

Serves 4

1 kg (2 lb) chuck steak, cut into 2.5 cm (1 inch) cubes

¼ teaspoon five spice powder

1 teaspoon pepper

2 lemon grass stalks, finely chopped

5 large garlic cloves, finely chopped

1 teaspoon salt

1 tablespoon dark soy sauce

2 teaspoons palm or golden granulated sugar

2 tablespoons vegetable oil

1 shallot, chopped

2 tomatoes, chopped

2 carrots, halved lengthways and cut into chunks

2 star anise

1 cinnamon stick

3 small green chillies, thinly sliced

600 ml (1 pint) water

basil leaves, to garnish

French bread, to serve

fish & seafood

Vietnam is a country that is criss-crossed with rivers and streams, tributaries and deltas as well as being bounded by the South China Sea. Fish and shellfish, both freshwater and saltwater, are abundant. Fish are also dried, which is an excellent way of preserving them in a country where ordinary people do not have refrigerators, and where the electricity supply can be eccentric. *Nuoc mam*, the ever-present fish sauce, is the highly nutritious result of thousands of tiny, fermented fish, and certainly there have been times in Vietnam's not too distant past when whole families have survived on not much more than a little rice with *nuoc mam* and a few wild edible plants.

hanoi fried halibut

cha ca hanoi

This dish is usually served in individual bowls over rice noodles.

1 Put the halibut into a bowl, add the fish sauce, salt and pepper and mix well. Cover and leave to marinate in the refrigerator for 2 hours.

2 Pour about 5 mm (¼ inch) of oil into a wok, swirl it around and heat it. Add the galangal, ginger and turmeric and stir, then add the chunks of halibut. Mix well and cook over a moderate heat for about 5 minutes, or until the fish is cooked through, stirring from time to time. Add the dill and mix in well.

3 Garnish the halibut with the spring onions, peanuts, coriander and basil and serve with the dipping sauce.

Serves 4

750 g (1½ lb) halibut, cut into 2.5 cm (1 inch) chunks

3 tablespoons Vietnamese fish sauce

1 teaspoon salt

1 teaspoon pepper

vegetable oil, for frying

2.5 cm (1 inch) piece of galangal, thinly sliced

5 cm (2 inch) piece of fresh root ginger, peeled and finely chopped

1 teaspoon ground turmeric

handful of dill, chopped

Nuoc Cham Dipping Sauce (see page 141), to serve

To garnish:

sliced spring onions

Crushed Roasted Peanuts (see page 141)

coriander and basil sprigs

caramel monkfish

ca caramen

1 Heat the oil in a wok, add the garlic and shallots and stir-fry for 1 minute. Add the monkfish and cook, stirring carefully, for 2–3 minutes, or until the fish has turned white.

2 Add the caramel syrup and stir to coat the fish. Add the fish sauce, water and pepper, stir and simmer gently for about 10 minutes, or until the fish is done and the sauce has slightly caramelized. To serve, garnish with the coriander leaves and sliced spring onions.

Serves 4

3 tablespoons vegetable oil

3 garlic cloves, finely chopped

3 shallots, finely chopped

750 g (1½ lb) monkfish, cut into chunks

4 tablespoons Caramel Syrup (see page 142)

4 tablespoons Vietnamese fish sauce

3 tablespoons water

½ teaspoon pepper

To garnish:

coriander leaves

sliced spring onions

deep-fried pomfret

ca xot ngot

1 Sift the rice flour, cornflour and sugar into a large bowl with a pinch of turmeric. Stir in the spring onions, egg whites and water and combine thoroughly to make a batter.

2 Heat the vegetable oil in a wok. Coat the pomfret fillets in the batter and fry them, in batches, for 5–10 minutes, until golden brown. Drain on kitchen paper and serve with the chilli sauce.

Serves 4

150 g (5 oz) rice flour

50 g (2 oz) cornflour

1 teaspoon caster sugar

pinch of ground turmeric

green parts of 2 spring onions, finely chopped

2 egg whites, whisked until frothy

125 ml (4 fl oz) cold water

vegetable oil, for deep-frying

4 pomfret, filleted

Quick Sweet Chilli Sauce (see page 142), to serve

crispy red snapper

ca ran

2 tablespoons vegetable oil

5 garlic cloves, finely chopped

3 large tomatoes, skinned, deseeded and chopped

3 small red chillies, finely sliced

60 g (2½ oz) palm or golden granulated sugar

4 tablespoons Vietnamese fish sauce

100 ml (3½ fl oz) water

vegetable oil, for frying

2 whole red snapper, each weighing 500–750 g (1–1½ lb), cleaned and scaled

To garnish:

chopped coriander leaves

sliced spring onion

1 Heat the oil in a heavy-based saucepan until moderately hot, add the garlic and stir-fry for about 30 seconds. Add the tomatoes and chillies and stir for 1 minute. Add the sugar, fish sauce and water and simmer, stirring occasionally, until the sauce has amalgamated and thickened. If it becomes too thick, you can add a little more water.

2 Heat about 1 cm (½ inch) of vegetable oil in a large frying pan. Put the snappers in the pan carefully, as the oil may spit, and cook over a moderate heat for about 15 minutes, without moving them. (If needs be, cut the heads off the fish in order to get them both in the pan.) They should get brown and crispy underneath. Turn the fish over carefully and cook for another 8–10 minutes. Remove from the pan and drain on kitchen paper.

3 Place the fish on a warmed serving dish. Reheat the sauce and pour it over the fish. Garnish with coriander leaves and spring onions.

Serves 4

shellfish in spicy tomato sauce

cau da

2 tablespoons vegetable oil

5 large garlic cloves, crushed and very finely chopped

2.5 cm (1 inch) piece of fresh root ginger, very finely chopped

500 g (1 lb) lobster meat

500 g (1 lb) queen scallops

4 tablespoons Vietnamese fish sauce

1 tablespoon palm sugar

1 small green chilli, finely sliced

2 ripe tomatoes, deseeded and chopped

2 spring onions, thinly sliced

chopped coriander leaves, to garnish

1 Heat the oil in a wok and stir-fry the garlic and ginger for 30 seconds. Add the lobster and scallops and fry carefully for about 1½–2 minutes, until the scallops have just cooked. Remove the shellfish to a plate.

2 Add the fish sauce, sugar and chilli, bring to the boil and cook, stirring, for 2 minutes. Add the tomatoes and spring onions, reduce the heat and simmer for 2 minutes, then return the shellfish to the wok. Heat through, then serve on a warmed platter, sprinkled with the coriander.

Serves 4–6

steamed clams

con nghieu hap

This is a simple, tasty recipe, which can be served with a more substantial rice or noodle dish. If you have difficulty finding clams, use mussels instead – they are equally good. If you find clams or mussels with shells that refuse to close while you are cleaning them, throw them away. Similarly, if you find any with shells that refuse to open during cooking, throw them away too.

1 Put the stock and lemon grass into a large saucepan and bring to the boil. Add the clams or mussels and cook, covered, for 4–5 minutes, or until the shells have opened. Remove from the heat, transfer to a warmed bowl and serve with the dipping sauce.

Serves 4

600 ml (1 pint) Fish Stock (see page 134)

6 lemon grass stalks, halved and crushed

1 kg (2 lb) clams or mussels, thoroughly cleaned

Nuoc Cham Dipping Sauce (see page 141), to serve

caramel prawns

tom rim

1 Heat the oil in a wok, add the garlic and chilli and stir-fry for about 30 seconds. Add the prawns and pepper and cook for about 1 minute. Add the salt and caramel syrup and cook for 1 further minute, stirring constantly.

2 To garnish, sprinkle with the coriander leaves and spring onions and serve with plain boiled rice.

Serves 4

1½ **tablespoons vegetable oil**

8 **garlic cloves, crushed and finely chopped**

1 **small red chilli, finely sliced**

500 g (1 lb) **raw prawns, peeled and deveined**

1 **teaspoon pepper**

½ **teaspoon salt**

1 **tablespoon Caramel Syrup (see page 142)**

boiled rice, to serve

To garnish:

chopped coriander leaves

thinly sliced spring onions

stuffed squid

muc nhoi thit

8–12 small squid, cleaned and dried

2 tablespoons vegetable oil

4 dried shiitake mushrooms, soaked and finely chopped

125 g (4 oz) boneless pork, finely minced

50 g (2 oz) rice vermicelli, soaked and cut into 1 cm (½ inch) lengths

2 shallots, finely chopped

2 garlic cloves, finely chopped

1 tablespoon finely chopped coriander stalks

6 pieces lily bud, soaked and chopped (optional)

1 small red chilli, finely sliced

½ teaspoon golden caster sugar

1 teaspoon salt

1 teaspoon pepper

chopped coriander leaves, to garnish

1 Remove the tentacles from the squid and chop them into small pieces.

2 Heat half of the oil in a wok, add the mushrooms, squid tentacles, pork, rice vermicelli, shallots, garlic, coriander stalks, lily buds (if using), red chilli, sugar, salt and pepper and stir-fry over a moderate heat until cooked. Remove from the wok and allow to cool.

3 Stuff each squid with some of the filling – do not fill them too full or they will burst – then close the tops with wooden cocktail sticks or sew with a needle and thread.

4 Heat the remaining oil in the wok and fry the stuffed squid fast over a high heat until opaque, just about 2–3 minutes. If you cook them much longer, the squid become rather rubbery. Allow the squid to cool slightly, then cut them into 1 cm (½ inch) slices and sprinkle with coriander leaves.

Serves 4

stuffed sea bass

cha bass

1 In a bowl, mix together the black fungus, mushrooms, spring onions, water chestnuts, ginger, rice vermicelli and sugar with 1 tablespoon of the soy sauce. Stuff the fish with the mixture and close the opening either with a long bamboo skewer or use a needle and thread.

2 Place the fish on a lightly oiled rack in a steamer. Pour over the remaining soy sauce, arrange the strips of chilli on the fish and drizzle the oil over them. Steam for 25 minutes, topping up the water level if necessary.

3 Remove the fish from the heat and leave to stand for 2–3 minutes. Transfer to a warmed platter and serve with rice and the dipping sauce.

Serves 4

4 dried black fungus, soaked and cut into strips

3 shiitake mushrooms, soaked and cut into strips

2 spring onions, finely sliced

60 g (2½ oz) water chestnuts, chopped

2.5 cm (1 inch) piece of fresh root ginger, finely chopped

30 g (1½ oz) rice vermicelli, soaked and cut into 2.5 cm (1 inch) lengths

2 teaspoons palm or light muscovado sugar

2 tablespoons dark soy sauce

2 x 750 g (1½ lb) sea bass, cleaned and scaled

1 long mild red chilli, shredded

2 tablespoons vegetable oil

To serve:

rice

Nuoc Cham Dipping Sauce (see page 141)

shellfish curry

cari do bien

Always be careful with mussels. Throw out any that remain open when you are cleaning them, and any that remain closed when you cook them.

1 Put the curry paste, cumin seeds, turmeric, coriander seeds, lemon grass, sugar and tomatoes in a mortar and pound, or process in a small food processor to make as smooth a paste as possible.

2 Heat the oil in a large wok and stir-fry the garlic, shallots and chillies for 2–3 minutes. Add the spice paste and continue to stir-fry for 3 minutes, then add the coconut milk, fish sauce and lime leaves. Mix well and simmer for 5 minutes. Finally, add the prawns, stirring, and then the mussels. Cover and simmer for a few minutes, until all the mussels are open. Garnish with coriander leaves and serve with rice.

Serves 4

1 heaped teaspoon Thai yellow curry paste

2 teaspoons cumin seeds, toasted and ground

1 teaspoon ground turmeric

1 teaspoon ground coriander seeds

1 lemon grass stalk, finely sliced

1 teaspoon palm sugar

5 ripe tomatoes, chopped

1 tablespoon vegetable oil

4 large garlic cloves, crushed and finely chopped

4 shallots, finely chopped

2 small red chillies, finely chopped

600 ml (1 pint) coconut milk

1 tablespoon Vietnamese fish sauce

6 kaffir lime leaves

375 g (12 oz) large raw prawns, peeled and deveined

1 kg (2 lb) mussels, scrubbed and debearded

coriander leaves, to garnish

boiled rice, to serve

desserts & drinks

Desserts as we know them are not generally eaten in Vietnam. Meals are most likely to be finished with a selection of different types of fabulous fresh fruit, if anything. Sweet snacks are available on the street all day long, however, and children and sweet-toothed adults find it hard to resist the banana and sweet potato fritters that are on offer. Sweet cakes, snacks and specialities such as coloured glutinous rice enclosing sweet bean paste, are also made for special occasions, Buddhist festivals and other celebrations. Drinks include refreshing Limeade (see page 130) and Vietnamese-style Coffee (see page 130), extremely strong and combined with condensed milk.

fresh fruit plate

trai cay

1 pineapple, peeled and cut
into chunks

2 mangoes, peeled and sliced

3 bananas, peeled, halved
lengthways and cut into 2.5 cm
(1 inch) pieces

4 lychees, peeled and pitted

2 limes, quartered

1 Arrange the fruit on a platter with the lime quarters around the edge, to squeeze over
the fruit according to taste.

Serves 6–8

caramelized bananas

chuoi caramen

4 bananas

60 g (2½ oz) hazelnuts, toasted
and ground

25 g (1 oz) fresh breadcrumbs

vegetable oil, for deep-frying

Sauce:

20 g (¾ oz) butter

150 g (5 oz) soft brown sugar

4 tablespoons water

300 ml (½ pint) coconut milk

1 Peel the bananas and cut them in half lengthways, then cut each piece in half again.
Mix together the hazelnuts and breadcrumbs in a dish and coat the banana pieces well,
pressing the crumbs on to them.

2 Heat together all the sauce ingredients in a small heavy-based saucepan, stirring all the
time until you have a caramel sauce.

3 Heat the oil in a deep-fryer or saucepan to 190°C (375°F) and fry the bananas in
batches, for 2 minutes, or until golden brown. Remove the bananas on to kitchen paper
to drain. To serve, place the bananas on individual dishes and pour over the warm
caramel sauce.

Serves 4

sticky rice with fruit coulis

gao nep voi trai cay cu li

This makes a rather unusual looking dessert. You can change the food colouring and the fruit according to season and taste. For example, you could use red colouring and make a lychee or kiwi fruit coulis, or you could leave the sticky rice white and make a mango coulis.

1 Drain the rice and put it into a heavy-based saucepan with the palm sugar, food colouring, if using, coconut milk and water and bring slowly to the boil. Reduce the heat and simmer until most of the liquid has been absorbed – the rice will firm up as it cools. Lightly oil 4 ramekins or moulds, press the rice into them and leave to cool.

2 Meanwhile, dry-fry the desiccated coconut until it is golden, and set aside to cool.

3 Process the strawberries and caster sugar in a food processor or blender.

4 Turn out the rice on to individual dessert plates, carefully pour the strawberry coulis around the edge, and sprinkle the tops with the toasted coconut.

Serves 4

250 g (8 oz) glutinous rice, soaked in water for 5–6 hours

3 tablespoons palm sugar, chopped

green food colouring (optional)

225 ml (7½ fl oz) coconut milk

375 ml (13 fl oz) water

vegetable oil, for brushing

60 g (2½ oz) desiccated coconut

375 g (12 oz) strawberries, hulled

60 g (2½ oz) golden caster sugar, or to taste

coconut crème caramel

dua kem caramen

125 g (4 oz) golden granulated sugar

100 ml (3½ fl oz) water

250 ml (8 fl oz) milk

250 ml (8 fl oz) coconut milk

4 eggs

60 g (2½ oz) golden caster sugar

½ teaspoon vanilla essence

To decorate:

1 tablespoon desiccated coconut, toasted

lime rind strips

1 Bring the granulated sugar and water to the boil in a heavy-based saucepan, stirring all the time to dissolve the sugar. Boil for 3–4 minutes, or until the mixture turns to a golden brown caramel syrup.

2 Remove from the heat and stir in 1 tablespoon of water if the mixture has become too thick. Pour the caramel syrup into 4 ramekins, swirling it around so that it coats the sides as well as lying at the bottom.

3 Pour the milk and the coconut milk into another saucepan, stir and heat until you can see small bubbles forming around the edge.

4 Meanwhile, beat the eggs in a mixing bowl with the caster sugar and vanilla essence. Remove the milk from the heat and pour it steadily over the egg mixture, whisking hard all the time.

5 Divide the mixture between the ramekins and place them on a rack in a roasting tin half filled with water. Bake in a preheated oven, 160°C (325°F), Gas Mark 3, for 40 minutes or until cooked.

6 Remove the ramekins from the oven and allow them to cool then run a knife around the edge of each one and turn out the crème caramels on to dessert plates. Sprinkle with the toasted desiccated coconut and lime rind strips before serving.

Serves 4

vietnamese-style coffee

ca phe viet nam

Both coffee and tea grow in Vietnam. Coffee is dark roasted, and served very strong. It is actually made using individual filters, but the main point is to make it very strong.

condensed milk
strong black coffee
ice cubes (optional)

1 Pour 2.5 cm (1 inch) condensed milk into a cup and add the same amount of very strong, black coffee. If you want to serve it cold, fill up the cup with ice cubes.

Serves 1

limeade

nuoc chanh

6 limes
125 g (4 oz) golden caster sugar
750 ml (1¼ pints) boiling water
pinch of salt
ice cubes
mint sprigs, to decorate

1 Halve the limes and squeeze the juice into a large jug. Put the squeezed halves into a heatproof jug with the sugar and water and leave to infuse for 15 minutes.

2 Add the salt to the infusion and give it a stir, then strain the infusion into the jug with the lime juice. Add a few ice cubes, cover and refrigerate.

3 To serve, place a few ice cubes in each glass and top up with the limeade. Decorate the glasses with mint sprigs.

Serves 1

basics

The food in Vietnam has been influenced by all the countries which surround it, China in particular. Generally speaking, Vietnamese food is not very chilli-hot, unlike Thai food. Instead, the Vietnamese go in for pungent dipping sauces, of which you can use as much or as little as you choose. You will always find Vietnamese fish sauce, *nuoc mam*, on the table, often made into a dipping sauce, Nuoc Cham (see page 141). Keep a stock of Crispy Fried Shallots (see page 139) in your storecupboard. You can quickly dry-fry them for use in cooking or as a garnish. As those who don't have a rice cooker will know, there are all sorts of different methods of cooking rice, and all sorts of different rice to be cooked. The method I have given in this chapter produces perfectly cooked Thai jasmine rice.

chicken stock

1.5 kg (3 lb) chicken backs, necks and wings, as skinless and fat free as possible

2.5 litres (4 pints) water

1 large onion

2 carrots

5 cm (1 inch) piece of fresh root ginger

1 teaspoon salt

You can make chicken stock by simply cooking chicken carcasses in water. You can also add many more ingredients, such as lemon grass and garlic. This version falls somewhere in between.

1 Put all the ingredients into a large saucepan or casserole and bring slowly to the boil. Reduce the heat and simmer, covered, for 2 hours, skimming the surface occasionally with a slotted spoon. Strain, without pressing the vegetables, and allow to cool.

2 If you refrigerate the stock overnight, any fat in it will rise to the surface and you will be able to remove it easily. You can use the stock you need immediately, and freeze the rest for the future.

Makes about 1.2 litres (2 pints)

fish stock

1.5 kg (3 lb) white fish trimmings, plus any available prawn heads and shells

6 black peppercorns

coriander stalks

1 lemon grass stalk, halved and crushed

2.5 litres (4 pints) water

Fish stock takes much less time to make than other stocks, and your fishmonger will often give you fish trimmings. Do not allow the stock to simmer for too long as overcooked bones can give it a rather gluey texture.

1 Put all the ingredients into a large saucepan and bring to the boil, skimming. Reduce the heat and simmer, covered, for 30 minutes.

2 Line a sieve with muslin then strain the stock. Freeze what you do not need immediately.

Makes about 1.5 litres (2½ pints)

beef stock

In Vietnam people often make a rich, spicy beef stock, using oxtails and adding star anise, cloves and other spices. For a plain beef stock, this recipe is all you need.

1 Put all the ingredients into a large saucepan or casserole and bring slowly to the boil, skimming when necessary. Boil hard for about 5 minutes, then reduce the heat. Simmer, covered, skimming occasionally, for 3 hours. Strain and allow to cool. Freeze what you do not need immediately.

Makes about 1.2 litres (2 pints)

1.5 kg (3 lb) beef bones, shin or neck

1 large onion, halved

2.5 cm (1 inch) piece of fresh root ginger

10 black peppercorns

1 teaspoon salt

3 litres (5 pints) water

vegetable stock

You can use almost any vegetable into a vegetable stock, but it is advisable not to put in too much cabbage or other strong green vegetables such as Brussels sprouts.

1 Put all the ingredients into a large saucepan and bring to the boil, then reduce the heat and simmer for 1 hour. Strain through a sieve, pressing the vegetables to release their juices.

2 This stock will last for several days in a covered container in the refrigerator or freeze what you do not need.

Makes about 1.5 litres (2½ pints)

3 large carrots, halved

2 onions, skins left on and washed

6 outside celery stalks, cut into 7 cm (3 inch) pieces

handful of parsley or coriander stalks and leaves

broccoli or cauliflower stalk

1 bay leaf

6 peppercorns

1 teaspoon salt

1 teaspoon sugar

2 litres (3½ pints) water

steamed rice

500 g (1 lb) Thai jasmine rice
1½–2 litres (2½–3½ pints) water

There are many different ways of cooking rice. I was taught this method in South-east Asia and it has always worked for me. You can cook the rice in advance if you like: leave it in a colander and, when you need it, steam it, covered, over a saucepan of boiling water. You can heat cooked rice from frozen this way too.

1 Rinse the rice in several changes of water to wash away the starch. Bring the water to the boil in a saucepan and add the rice. Return it to the boil, stirring to break up any clumps that may form. Boil for 3–4 minutes, then strain through a colander.

2 Place the colander over another saucepan of boiling water, making sure that the water level is well below the rice. Take a chopstick and make a few steam holes in the rice by pushing the chopstick through until it meets the colander. Put a saucepan lid over the colander – not touching the rice – and steam for about 15 minutes. Remove the lid shortly before serving and fluff up the rice with a fork.

Serves 4

glutinous rice

500 g (1 lb) glutinous rice

Often known as sticky rice, this can be used in place of ordinary rice or sweetened for a dessert. In Vietnam it is normally eaten for breakfast or in the evening, but not at lunchtime. It is often steamed in bamboo rice steamers, which can be obtained in various sizes from individual to family size.

1 Soak the rice in a large bowl of water for 8 hours. Drain the rice and rinse it under running water.

2 Line a steamer with muslin and spread the rice over it. Steam, covered, for 30–40 minutes. Taste the rice after 20 minutes to check the consistency: it should be softish at this stage. You can always sprinkle a little water over it to help it along.

Serves 4

pork crackling

Like crispy shallots and crushed roasted peanuts, these little bits of crackling are lovely to throw on to fried rice, noodle soups or anything else that needs a finishing touch. Ask your butcher to score the pork rind as he would for crackling on a roast.

500 g (1 lb) pork rind

1 Roast the rind in a preheated oven, 190–200°C (375–400°F), Gas Mark 5–6, for 10 minutes, keeping your eye on it after that. The fat should render and the skin become crispy. Remove and leave to cool on kitchen paper. Cut the rind into short pieces and store what you do not want immediately in an airtight container. It will last for at least 2 weeks.

Makes 375 g (12 oz)

prawn crackers

vegetable oil, for deep-frying
1 box uncooked prawn crackers

We have all eaten prawn crackers in oriental restaurants, and they make a great snack. They are also easy and good fun to cook and, like most things, taste so much better when they have just been made. It is best to cook them in a small saucepan as you cannot deal with too many of them at once.

1 Heat about 7 cm (3 inches) of oil in a small saucepan. When it is good and hot, pop 1 uncooked piece from the box into the oil. It should almost immediately blossom into a prawn cracker 2–3 times its original size. Remove it immediately with a slotted spoon or bamboo sieve to drain on kitchen paper. If you are not careful, it will burn. Add the remaining crackers, a few at a time, until they are all cooked.

Serves 4

crispy fried shallots

These crispy shallots are another delicious garnish that enhances just about everything. They will keep for 3–4 weeks in an airtight container, so it is worth making a large quantity. In Vietnam the thinly sliced fresh shallots would be spread out in single layer and dried in the sun for several hours, which shortens the amount of frying time.

1 Heat the oil in a frying pan until it is good and hot. Add the shallots and cook until they are brown and crisp, 5–10 minutes. Remove and drain on kitchen paper. You may need to cook the shallots in batches as they cook best if they are in a single layer.

Makes 375 g (12 oz)

125 ml (4 fl oz) vegetable oil
12 large shallots, thinly sliced

lime & ginger sauce

1 Put the ginger, sugar, chillies and garlic into a mortar and pound until blended well. Add the lime segments and pound again until the mixture is as smooth as possible, then stir in the fish sauce. If you like, you can use a small food processor instead of a pestle and mortar.

2 This sauce will keep for up to 10 days in an airtight container in the refrigerator.

Serves 4

2.5 cm (1 inch) piece of fresh root ginger, finely chopped

2 tablespoons palm or golden caster sugar

2 small red chillies, finely chopped, or ½ teaspoon crushed dried chillies

2 large garlic cloves, crushed

1 lime, divided into segments

2 tablespoons Vietnamese fish sauce

crushed roasted peanuts

You will find crushed roasted peanuts on the table almost everywhere you go in Vietnam. They are used as a garnish on soups, noodles, rice dishes – almost everything.

1 Dry-fry the nuts gently in a frying pan or spread them out on a baking tray and put them in a preheated oven, 140–150°C (275–300°F), Gas Mark 1–2. Stir them around until they turn a golden colour. Remove and allow to cool.

2 Place the nuts in a plastic bag and crush them with a rolling pin. They will keep for up to 4 weeks in an airtight container in the refrigerator.

Makes 50 g (2 oz)

50 g (2 oz) skinless unroasted peanuts

nuoc cham dipping sauce

1 Put the sugar in a bowl and pour the hot water over it, stirring until it is completely dissolved. Add all the other ingredients, stir well and allow to cool to room temperature.

2 This dipping sauce can be kept in an airtight container in the refrigerator for up to 7 days.

Makes 500 ml (17 fl oz)

125 g (4 oz) palm or golden caster sugar

250 ml (8 fl oz) hot water

125 ml (4 fl oz) Vietnamese fish sauce

1 tablespoon white rice vinegar

60 ml (2½ fl oz) lime juice

2–4 small red or green chillies, finely chopped

3–5 large garlic cloves, finely chopped

caramel syrup

125 g (4 oz) palm or golden granulated sugar

150 ml (¼ pint) water

1 Bring the sugar and water to the boil in a small heavy-based saucepan and cook for about 3 minutes, stirring, or until the sauce becomes syrupy. Remove the saucepan from the heat, add a little more cold water, and pour into a heatproof container.

2 This sauce will keep, covered, in the refrigerator for about 10 days.

Makes 175 ml (6 fl oz)

quick sweet chilli sauce

150 ml (¼ pint) mild sweet chilli sauce

2 tablespoons light soy sauce

2 tablespoons red rice vinegar

1 tablespoon palm sugar

125 ml (4 fl oz) Chicken Stock (see page 134) or Vegetable Stock (see page 135)

2 teaspoons cornflour

50 ml (2 fl oz) cold water

60 g (2½ oz) coriander leaves, chopped

1 Combine the chilli sauce, soy sauce, vinegar, sugar and stock in a small heavy-based saucepan over a moderate heat. Mix together the cornflour and water and add to the sauce, then stir until the sauce thickens and comes to the boil. Add the coriander leaves just before serving.

Makes about 450 ml (¾ pint)

easy peanut sauce

1 Heat the oil in a heavy-based saucepan, add the garlic, shallot and chillies and fry gently for 2 minutes or until the shallots are softening.

2 Add the peanut butter, sugar, fish sauce and coconut milk and mix together thoroughly, then cook over a low heat for 10–15 minutes. Add more coconut milk if the sauce is becoming too thick.

Serves 4

1 tablespoon groundnut oil

2 garlic cloves, crushed and finely chopped

1 shallot, finely chopped

2–3 small red chillies, finely chopped

125 g (4 oz) crunchy peanut butter

2 tablespoons palm sugar

2 tablespoons Vietnamese fish sauce

150 ml (¼ pint) coconut milk, plus extra if necessary

cucumber dipping sauce

1 Put all the ingredients into a bowl and mix together well. Season to taste with salt and pepper.

2 This dipping sauce will keep for several days in a refrigerator, in an airtight container.

Serves 6–8

½ cucumber, peeled, deseeded and grated

juice of 2 limes

50 ml (2 fl oz) cold water

2 tablespoons Vietnamese fish sauce

1 small red chilli, finely chopped

1 large garlic clove, finely chopped

½–1 teaspoon golden caster sugar

salt and pepper

index